A COMPREHENSIVE COMMENTARY ON THE HEART SUTRA (*PRAJÑĀPĀRAMITĀ-HṚDAYA-SŪTRA*)

BDK English Tripiṭaka 66-I

A COMPREHENSIVE COMMENTARY ON THE HEART SUTRA (*PRAJÑĀPĀRAMITA-HṚDAYA-SŪTRA*)

Translated from the Chinese of K'uei-chi
(Taishō Volume 33, Number 1710)

by

Heng-ching Shih

in collaboration with
Dan Lusthaus

Numata Center
for Buddhist Translation and Research
2001

First Printing, 2001
ISBN: 1-886439-11-7
Library of Congress Catalog Card Number: 99-75897

Published by
Numata Center for Buddhist Translation and Research
2620 Warring Street
Berkeley, California 94704

Printed in the United States of America

A Message on the Publication of the English Tripiṭaka

The Buddhist canon is said to contain eighty-four thousand different teachings. I believe that this is because the Buddha's basic approach was to prescribe a different treatment for every spiritual ailment, much as a doctor prescribes a different medicine for every medical ailment. Thus his teachings were always appropriate for the particular suffering individual and for the time at which the teaching was given, and over the ages not one of his prescriptions has failed to relieve the suffering to which it was addressed.

Ever since the Buddha's Great Demise over twenty-five hundred years ago, his message of wisdom and compassion has spread throughout the world. Yet no one has ever attempted to translate the entire Buddhist canon into English throughout the history of Japan. It is my greatest wish to see this done and to make the translations available to the many English-speaking people who have never had the opportunity to learn about the Buddha's teachings.

Of course, it would be impossible to translate all of the Buddha's eighty-four thousand teachings in a few years. I have, therefore, had one hundred thirty-nine of the scriptural texts in the prodigious Taishō edition of the Chinese Buddhist canon selected for inclusion in the First Series of this translation project.

It is in the nature of this undertaking that the results are bound to be criticized. Nonetheless, I am convinced that unless someone takes it upon himself or herself to initiate this project, it will never be done. At the same time, I hope that an improved, revised edition will appear in the future.

It is most gratifying that, thanks to the efforts of more than a hundred Buddhist scholars from the East and the West, this monumental project has finally gotten off the ground. May the rays of the Wisdom of the Compassionate One reach each and every person in the world.

NUMATA Yehan
Founder of the English
Tripiṭaka Project

August 7, 1991

Editorial Foreword

In January 1982, Dr. NUMATA Yehan, the founder of the Bukkyō Dendō Kyōkai (Society for the Promotion of Buddhism), decided to begin the monumental task of translating the complete Taishō edition of the Chinese Tripiṭaka (Buddhist canon) into the English language. Under his leadership, a special preparatory committee was organized in April 1982. By July of the same year, the Translation Committee of the English Tripiṭaka was officially convened.

The initial Committee consisted of the following members: (late) HANAYAMA Shōyū (Chairperson), BANDŌ Shōjun, ISHIGAMI Zennō, KAMATA Shigeo, KANAOKA Shūyū, MAYEDA Sengaku, NARA Yasuaki, (late) SAYEKI Shinkō, (late) SHIOIRI Ryōtatsu, TAMARU Noriyoshi, (late) TAMURA Kwansei, URYŪZU Ryūshin, and YUYAMA Akira. Assistant members of the Committee were as follows: KANAZAWA Atsushi, WATANABE Shōgo, Rolf Giebel of New Zealand, and Rudy Smet of Belgium.

After holding planning meetings on a monthly basis, the Committee selected one hundred thirty-nine texts for the First Series of translations, an estimated one hundred printed volumes in all. The texts selected are not necessarily limited to those originally written in India but also include works written or composed in China and Japan. While the publication of the First Series proceeds, the texts for the Second Series will be selected from among the remaining works; this process will continue until all the texts, in Japanese as well as in Chinese, have been published.

Frankly speaking, it will take perhaps one hundred years or more to accomplish the English translation of the complete Chinese and Japanese texts, for they consist of thousands of works. Nevertheless, as Dr. NUMATA wished, it is the sincere hope of the Committee that this project will continue unto completion, even after all its present members have passed away.

It must be mentioned here that the final object of this project is not academic fulfillment but the transmission of the teaching of the

Buddha to the whole world in order to create harmony and peace among humankind. To that end, the translators have been asked to minimize the use of explanatory notes of the kind that are indispensable in academic texts, so that the attention of general readers will not be unduly distracted from the primary text. Also, a glossary of selected terms is appended to aid in understanding the text.

To my great regret, however, Dr. NUMATA passed away on May 5, 1994, at the age of ninety-seven, entrusting his son, Mr. NUMATA Toshihide, with the continuation and completion of the Translation Project. The Committee also lost its able and devoted Chairperson, Professor HANAYAMA Shōyū, on June 16, 1995, at the age of sixty-three. After these severe blows, the Committee elected me, Vice President of Musashino Women's College, to be the Chair in October 1995. The Committee has renewed its determination to carry out the noble intention of Dr. NUMATA, under the leadership of Mr. NUMATA Toshihide.

The present members of the Committee are MAYEDA Sengaku (Chairperson), BANDŌ Shōjun, ISHIGAMI Zennō, ICHISHIMA Shōshin, KAMATA Shigeo, KANAOKA Shūyū, NARA Yasuaki, TAMARU Noriyoshi, URYŪZU Ryūshin, YUYAMA Akira, Kenneth K. Tanaka, WATANABE Shōgo; and assistant member YONEZAWA Yoshiyasu.

The Numata Center for Buddhist Translation and Research was established in November 1984, in Berkeley, California, U.S.A., to assist in the publication of the BDK English Tripiṭaka First Series. In December 1991, the Publication Committee was organized at the Numata Center, with Professor Philip Yampolsky as the Chairperson. To our sorrow, Professor Yampolsky passed away in July 1996. In February 1997, Dr. Kenneth K. Inada became Chair and served in that capacity until August 1999. The current Chair, Dr. Francis H. Cook, has been continuing the work since October 1999. All of the remaining texts will be published under the supervision of this Committee, in close cooperation with the Editorial Committee in Tokyo.

MAYEDA Sengaku
Chairperson
Editorial Committee of
the BDK English Tripiṭaka

Publisher's Foreword

The Publication Committee shares with the Editorial Committee the responsibility of realizing the vision of Dr. Yehan Numata, founder of Bukkyō Dendō Kyōkai, the Society for the Promotion of Buddhism. This vision is no less than to make the Buddha's teaching better known throughout the world, through the translation and publication in English of the entire collection of Buddhist texts compiled in the *Taishō Shinshū Daizōkyō,* published in Tokyo in the early part of the twentieth century. This huge task is expected to be carried out by several generations of translators and may take as long as a hundred years to complete. Ultimately, the entire canon will be available to anyone who can read English and who wishes to learn more about the teaching of the Buddha.

The present generation of staff members of the Publication Committee are Diane Ames, Marianne Dresser, Eisho Nasu, Koh Nishiike, and Reverend Kiyoshi Yamashita, president of the Numata Center for Buddhist Translation and Research, Berkeley, California. The Publication Committee is headquartered at the Numata Center and, working in close cooperation with the Editorial Committee, is responsible for the usual tasks associated with preparing translations for publication.

In October 1999, I became the third chairperson of the Publication Committee, on the retirement of its very capable former chair, Dr. Kenneth K. Inada. The Committee is devoted to the advancement of the Buddha's teaching through the publication of excellent translations of the thousands of texts that make up the Buddhist canon.

Francis H. Cook
Chairperson
Publication Committee

Contents

Translator's Introduction

The *Pan-jo po-lo-mi-to hsin-ching yu-tsan* is a comprehensive commentary on the *Heart Sutra* (*Prajñāpāramitā-hṛdaya-sūtra*) by K'uei-chi (632–682). The *Heart Sutra,* a Buddhist classic and the most popular sutra in China, comprises only two hundred and sixty-two words in the Chinese translation. However, it is said that the essence of the *Prajñāpāramitā Sutra,* and even the entire Mahayana teaching, is contained within it.

The *Heart Sutra,* which belongs to the voluminous Prajñāpāramitā literature, has been translated repeatedly into different languages throughout Buddhist history. The Japanese scholar Hariba Gensui, in his edition of the *Heart* scripture (*Hannya shin-gyō ihon taisei*), lists all known versions in all languages used: Sanskrit, Chinese, Tibetan, Japanese, English, etc. In China, there are over a hundred commentaries on the *Heart Sutra* based on various Buddhist doctrinal systems.

The *Heart Sutra* concisely elucidates the philosophy of *śūnyatā* (emptiness), which teaches that not only the self (*ātman*) but also all dharmas—the elements that make up our world—are empty and ultimately nonexistent. The fact that all things in the phenomenal world are constantly changing indicates that they are devoid of inherent self-nature (*svabhāva*). The reason that they are without selfhood is because they arise in dependence on causes and conditions (*pratītyasamutpāda*). Insight into the empty nature of everything leads to the perfection of wisdom (*prajñāpāramitā*). This is the message the *Heart Sutra* is conveying. The soteriological significance of *śūnyatā* lies in the fact that with the realization of emptiness one is able to eradicate attachments to the supposed reality of the self and dharmas. As a result, one can undertake spiritual endeavors egolessly.

K'uei-chi, one of the most important Buddhist scholars of the early T'ang dynasty, is also known as Tz'u-en, an appellation derived from the name of his residence, Ta-tz'u-en Monastery. He was the most outstanding disciple of the renowned pilgrim Hsüan-tsang and founded the Fa-hsiang school, the Chinese version of the Indian Yogācāra school of Buddhism. K'uei-chi made commentaries on many Yogācāra treatises translated by his master Hsüan-tsang. These treatises became the fundamental texts of the school and are very important sources and references for understanding Fa-hsiang doctrines.

The *Sung kao-seng ch'uan (Sung Biographies of Eminent Monks)* compiled by Tsan-ning contains the longest, although not necessarily the most reliable, biography of K'uei-chi. His well-known nickname, "Three-Cart Monk," is taken from the story of Hsüan-tsang's initial contact with K'uei-chi, who traveled with three carts bearing his entertainers, female servants, and delicacies. Hsüan-tsang was impressed by K'uei-chi's superior intelligence and urged him to become a monk. K'uei-chi refused, only later consenting to join the order on the condition that he be exempted from keeping the five cardinal precepts. The *Sung kao-seng chuan* states that K'uei-chi finally gave up his worldly desires on the advice of an old man who was none other than an embodiment of the Bodhisattva Mañjuśrī. However, this story is in conflict with K'uei-chi's own autobiographical account, in which he states that since his youth he had longed for the religious life and that he became detached from worldly desires quite early.

One possible explanation for these conflicting accounts is that the "Three-Cart" nickname may derive from another source. Stanley Weinstein, in his "A Biographical Study of Tz'u-en" (*Monumenta Nipponica,* 15, 1–2 [1959] 119–49), proposed a very reasonable hypothesis for the use of the nickname, suggesting that "Three-Cart" was derived from K'uei-chi's unconventional interpretation of the *Lotus Sutra*. K'uei-chi asserted that the parable of the three carts, symbolizing the three vehicles, represents the ultimate truth of Buddhism, instead of the doctrine of the all-embracing one vehicle (*ekayāna*) advocated in the *Lotus Sutra.*

Aside from his commentaries on Yogācāra texts, K'uei-chi also commented on and reinterpreted many non-Yogācāra works, such as the *Lotus Sutra,* the *Vimalakīrtinirdeśa Sutra,* and the *Heart Sutra,* from a Yogācāra viewpoint. The *Pan-jo po-lo-mi-to hsin-ching yu-tsan* is especially significant and unique in that K'uei-chi commented on the *Heart Sutra* from both Madhyamikan and Yogācārin perspectives. Thus, it became the only source of the Fa-hsiang school's view of Prajñāpāramitā thought.

The commentary can be roughly divided into two main parts. The first part expounds the meaning of the title, *Prajñāpāramitā-hṛdaya-sūtra,* and goes on to describe the teachings and practice of the six perfections (*pāramitā*s) of the bodhisattva. The second part begins with an explanation of the bodhisattva stages (*bhūmi*s) and then gives a detailed elucidation of the text of the *Heart Sutra,* sentence by sentence. It first explains the meaning of *practice* by citing the five stages of practice as taught by the Yogācāra school, the ten perfections (*pāramitā*s), the thirteen abodes, etc. It goes on to explain the meaning and negate the reality of the characteristics of dharmas (*dharma-lakṣaṇa*s), such as the five *skandha*s, the twelve sense fields, the eighteen realms, and the Four Noble Truths. Finally, it expounds the religious significance of the perfection of wisdom.

Throughout this commentary, K'uei-chi quotes from a wide variety of texts in explaining the meaning of particular passages. Readers familiar with the *Yogācārabhūmi-śāstra,* the *Ch'eng wei-shih lun* (Taishō 1585; published as *Demonstration of Consciousness Only* in the volume entitled *Three Texts on Consciousness Only,* translated by Francis H. Cook, Numata Center, 1999), the *Viṃśatikā* (Taishō 1590; published as *The Treatise in Twenty Verses on Consciousness Only* in *Three Texts on Consciousness Only,* op. cit.), the *Madhyāntavibhāga-śāstra,* and related texts will thus have a better understanding of this commentary.

In addition, there are several subcommentaries on this commentary, of which the *Pan-jo hsin ching yu-tsan k'ung-t'ung chi* by Shou-ch'ien and the *Hannya shingyō yū-san shō* by Ze-a are the most extensive.

A COMPREHENSIVE COMMENTARY ON THE HEART SUTRA (*PRAJÑĀPĀRAMITĀ-HṚDAYA-SŪTRA*)

by

K'uei-chi

Part One

Commentary: Sentient beings, hindered by afflictions, respectfully accept deviant teachings, slander the Mahayana, and interpret literally the doctrines of emptiness and existence as taught in the sutras. Following their understanding of the printed words, they develop aversions and attachments. If they wish to understand the essence of the teachings, they must follow worthy [beneficial] spiritual friends because many confused teachers give erroneous teachings. Discouraged by the extensive and abstruse wording of the sutras, people lose interest in them. Although fond of shorter sutras, they cannot understand them. They take ultimate and conventional truth to refer to the existence or nonexistence of the dharmas of mind and sense objects (*viṣaya*); these then give rise to conceptualizations which they either cling to or deny. 523b10

In order to thoroughly elucidate the meaning of the true Dharma and to distinguish the true and the false so as to benefit sentient beings who have faith and who study, I will briefly comment on the Middle Way as I understand it.

In the *Saṃdhinirmocana-sūtra,* through the doctrine on the mere imaginary nature (*parikalpita*) [of all dharmas], the Buddha taught that all dharmas are without self-nature (*niḥsvabhāva*), neither arising nor ceasing, and are originally marks of nirvana; this constitutes a competent interpretation of the three kinds of non–self-natures. At that time Paramārthajāta (Sheng-yi-sheng) Bodhisattva said to the Buddha,

> The World-honored One, the Buddha, turned the wheel of the Four Noble Truths for those working toward the realization of a *śrāvaka*. Although rare and wonderful, the Four Noble Truths were not the ultimate teaching and became the source of various disputes. Later, the Buddha turned the "secret wheel" for the Mahayanists, expounding that all dharmas are without self-nature, production and extinction,

> and are originally nothing other than nirvana. It seems the meaning of this [teaching], though even more wonderful, was not yet understood and also became the source of disputes. For the sake of the aspirants of all vehicles, the Buddha then turned the wheel disclosing understanding to expound those unsurpassed, comprehensive, and ultimate teachings of full revelation of the whole truth, which will not become a source of disputes.

The *Suvarṇaprabhāsa-sūtra* (*Golden Light Sutra*) calls these three turnings [of the wheel] "transforming," "illuminating," and "maintaining," for they cut through designation and have [the functions of] negation and affirmation. Because sentient beings, confused about the true marks of things, engage in deluded actions
523c and flounder in the ocean of cyclic existence (i.e., samsara), the Holy Dharma King, having realized the nature of dharmas, employed skillful means to correspond to [the varying] capacities of sentient beings by expounding in words the Dharma that is beyond words, in order to help them attain the truth of the Middle Way. A verse says:

> Sometimes the Buddhas speak of self,
> Other times they speak of no-self.
> All phenomena are in reality
> Neither self nor no-self.

Other sutras also say that the Buddha used one voice to convey boundless teachings and that different sentient beings comprehended them differently according to their own capabilities. Just as a drum makes sounds, or a *maṇi* jewel rains down treasures upon request, so the Buddha set forth various kinds of teachings in response to the [different] capacities of individuals. [The Buddha's immediate followers had] intelligent and compatible views and did not engage in disputes; nevertheless, after the Buddha's nirvana, on account of Mahādeva, disputes concerning the self and dharmas arose. At first, attachment to existence was prevalent. A verse says:

Rely on the teaching of the noble truth.
Carefully reflect on the teaching of the Buddha, and
Just as one distinguishes gold from sand,
So distinguish and hold to the truth.

To eradicate attachment to existence, the venerable Nāgārjuna and others gathered true teachings to elucidate the purport of emptiness. For example, a verse says:

The true nature of conditioned things is empty
For [such things are] illusory and dependently arisen.
Unconditioned things also lack substantial reality,
For they are unsubstantial like flowers in the sky.

This is to say that on the level of conventional truth all dharmas are existent, while according to the ultimate truth all are empty. However, the nature of true emptiness is neither empty nor existent; it is only from the perspective of ultimate truth that the nature of all dharmas is seen as emptiness. From this teaching, beings develop [an erroneous] view of emptiness. Thus, the Bodhisattva Asaṅga requested Maitreya to expound the teaching on the Middle Way so as to eliminate both attachments [to existence and to emptiness]. A verse says:

[The mind that] falsely discriminates exists;
Both [the self and dharmas] lack true existence.
In this [false discrimination] there is only emptiness,
but in that [emptiness], there are also these [self and
dharmas].

Therefore, it is said that all dharmas
Are neither empty nor non-empty.
Yet because there are non-being and being,
This accords with the Middle Way.

This is to say that conventionally self and dharmas exist, while ultimately both are empty. However, in order to eliminate clinging to emptiness or existence, the Buddha claimed that all dharmas are

both existent and empty, or that they are neither empty nor exis-
524a tent. The nature of designations is free from the dual faults of existence and emptiness. From the perspective of ultimate truth, both emptiness and existence are asserted. Hence, Maitreya said that the conditioned and the unconditioned are said to exist; the self and its possessions are said to be empty. Nevertheless, this does not mean that what exists or is empty is truly empty or existent. According to the Buddha's teachings, there is no contradiction between existence and emptiness. Since the Dharma is free from intellectual interpretation, how can there [ultimately] be existence or emptiness? It is to eradicate afflictions in accordance with the malady that existence and emptiness are expediently expounded. The followers of later generations grew attached to words and assumed that what they understood was in agreement with the Middle Way and that what others understood was erroneous.

Now I shall comment on the meaning of the *Heart Sutra* in order to explain both points of view. Intelligent people should be able to distinguish what is right and wrong concerning the profound doctrine.

Prajñāpāramitā is the general title for the *Mahāprajñāpāramitā-sūtra,* while the *Heart Sutra* (*Prajñāpāramitā-hṛdaya-sūtra*) is one particular sutra found within it. It is the heart of the *Prajñāpāramitā-sūtra.* Of the six interpretations of compound terms *ṣaṭ-samāsa,* [*prajñāpāramitā-hṛdaya*] is a *tatpuruṣa.* Of the cases (*subanta*), it is the genitive. The *Heart Sutra* is also called "*Prajñāpāramitā-sūtra,*" but since Prajñāpāramitā is the name of a collection and this is one particular sutra, it is [properly] designated the *Heart Sutra.*

Prajñā means wisdom. Traditionally it has three meanings: (1) the metaphysical meaning—"true principle," (2) the contemplative meaning—"true wisdom," and (3) the literary meaning—"true teachings." Here five meanings may be given: [the three mentioned above, plus] (4) a meaning of "retinue"—"innumerable practices," and (5) a meaning of "field of sense objects" (*viṣaya-gocara*)—"all dharmas." *Prajñā* means to cultivate both blessings and wisdom in order to comprehend [the meanings of] both existence and emptiness. It includes both searching for and understanding the nature of wisdom and the form of wisdom. It can eradicate negative habit patterns and bring forth realization of the true nature of dharmas. It is foremost among countless virtues and the guide to innumerable practices. Although it primarily refers to wisdom, it encompasses all other dharmas.

Pāra means the other shore. Traditionally it refers to *bodhi* and nirvana. Here it is explained in five aspects: (1) *jñeya* (i.e., what has been made known through some means of knowledge); (2) teachings; (3) principles; (4) practices; and (5) results. *Mitā* means "leaving" or "reaching." Through the practice of wisdom, one leaves behind defilements, exhausts [the clinging to] phenomenal existence and emptiness. Thoroughly comprehending the six treasures (i.e., the Tripiṭaka of both the Mahayana and the Hinayana), one understands conventional and ultimate truth, accomplishes the two causes in deeds, achieves enlightenment and nirvana, and thus reaches the other shore. Both the essence and functioning [of wisdom] are manifest; thus, it is called *"mitā."* However, only when the practice is accompanied by the seven excellences can it be called *"pāramitā"* (perfection). The seven excellences are: (1) abiding in the bodhisattva nature (*gotra*), (2) relying on the aspiration for enlightenment (*bodhicitta*); (3) having compassion for sentient beings; (4) thoroughly cultivating various deeds; (5) having insight into non-form; (6) transferring [merit] for enlightenment; and (7) not being defiled by the two hindrances. Lacking any of these seven excellences, the practice of wisdom cannot be called reaching the other shore. The first *kalpa* [of a bodhisattva's progress to Buddhahood] is called *"pāramitā."* The second *kalpa* is called "an intermediate *pāramitā,*" and the third *kalpa* is "a great *pāramitā.*" In the stage of Buddhahood, there is no other name given. Since *prajñāpāramitā* encompasses both cause and effect, the general designation *"prajñāpāramitā"* is used.

Heart (*hṛdaya*) signifies essence and excellence. Because the *Mahāprajñāpāramitā-sūtra* is voluminous and extensive in

meaning, those who receive, uphold, transmit, or study it may easily become discouraged. Therefore the sages, for the purpose of propagating the Dharma, captured the supreme essence by composing this condensed sutra. Consequently, the three divisions and the two prefaces [that usually appear in a sutra] were left out. The most subtle and essential elements [of the *Mahāprajñāpāramitā-sūtra*] were selected as the main points to be mentioned. Although this sutra contains various teachings, it mainly articulates that form itself is emptiness. It encompasses thousands of doctrines, running through the principle of "no knowledge" to that of attainment. It explores the profound purpose of the *Mahāprajñāpāramitā-sūtra* and eluci-
524b dates its essence. Hence it is called "heart."

Sutra is a guiding explanation concerning profound principles and an enduring example that guides confused beings. In order to enlighten [sentient beings], this sutra was taught in accordance with the essence, [that is, the core or "heart,"] of wisdom. Therefore, it has *Heart* as its title. Likewise, the *Yogācārabhūmi-śāstra,* the *Daśabhūmika-sūtra,* and other sutras [that elucidate the stages (*bhūmis*) of practice] make up their titles.

SUTRA: KUAN-TZU-TSAI (AVALOKITEŚVARA) BODHISATTVA,

Commentary: The Madhyamikans comment that this passage can be divided into two parts: *Kuan-tzu-tsai* means to eliminate two types of attachment and to reveal two types of emptiness, while *bodhisattva* means to praise two kinds of reliance and to obtain two types of benefits.

The *Mahāprajñāpāramitā-sūtra* says:

> The Buddha said to Śāriputra, "When a bodhisattva *mahāsattva* is practicing the perfection of wisdom, he or she should contemplate the fact that a true bodhisattva does not perceive a truly existent bodhisattva nor perceive the name of a truly existent bodhisattva because a bodhisattva is empty of self-nature, and the name 'bodhisattva' is also empty."

Here *bodhisattva* is elucidated so that beings will not perceive [an existent self]. For the purpose of breaking attachment to self, it is said that the self is empty.

The Yogācārins comment that this sutra has three parts. First, Kuan-tzu-tsai (Avalokiteśvara) is pointed out as a supreme person for his practices so as to exhort others and produce in them the aspiration for enlightenment. Then Śāriputra represents the person who responds [to the teachings] and serves as an example. Finally, *bodhisattva* shows the virtue of study and praises the supreme benefit obtained [from the practice of wisdom].

[An alternative interpretation is that] the first part means to encourage the disciple; the second part, to eradicate the four barriers; and the third part, to leave behind suffering and to realize perfect enlightenment. Encouragement has three aspects. The sutra shows that the bodhisattva first practices and then exhorts others to develop their own aspiration. This is the first encouragement. That is, when a person hears that enlightenment is vast and profound and gives rise to the thought of retrogressing, he should encourage himself thus:

> "When Kuan-tzu-tsai first brought forth his aspiration, he was full of afflictions, but he developed confidence arising from the shell of ignorance. He gave up his life and wealth in order to seek the wisdom of enlightenment. Being extremely diligent, he realized perfect enlightenment. Likewise, I should encourage myself to heroically increase my practice like him, without belittling myself or retrogressing."

Kuan means being aware in order to impart wisdom and compassion. *Tzu-tsai* means not stagnating, which has the wondrous function of liberating others. When all beings purify the three actions (i.e., of body, speech, and mind) and take refuge in Kuan-tzu-tsai, he responds to their prayers and bestows aid through his six supernatural powers (*abhijñā*). Disregarding suffering, he averts disasters with his miraculous activities. Serving as a friend who manifests even without supplication, he cures illnesses according to the affliction. As his benefit is difficult to conceive, he is called "Kuan-tzu-tsai."

Kuan also means illumination, that is, insight into emptiness and existence. *Tzu-tsai* means freedom, which is the final result obtained from one's previous practice of the six perfections. After practicing wisdom and contemplation, [Kuan-tzu-tsai] perfects the ten kinds of *mastery* (i.e., the common meaning of *tzu-tsai* in Chinese): (1) mastery of lifespan—the ability to prolong life; (2) mastery of the mind—not being defiled by birth and death; (3) mastery of wealth—treasures appear as desired as the outcome of the practice of generosity; (4) mastery of action—performing virtuous deeds and exhorting others to do likewise; (5) mastery of birth—the ability obtained through the practice of the precepts to transform [oneself and things] as desired; (6) mastery of supreme understanding—the ability resulting from the practice of patience to transform [oneself and things] as desired; (7) mastery of aspiration—wishes are realized as conceptualized and attainment achieved due
524c to the practice of effort; (8) mastery of supernatural powers—the most excellent supernatural powers are achieved through the practice of meditation; (9) mastery of knowledge—the knowledge of words and sounds; and (10) mastery of the Dharma—comprehension of the sutras obtained through the practice of wisdom.

Kuan-tzu-tsai Bodhisattva has attained that perfect awakening which is the stage just prior to Buddhahood. There is no darkness that he does not illuminate; therefore, he is called "Kuan-tzu-tsai." To call him Kuan-yin ("Contemplating Sounds") would be to misinterpret the term and to lose the meaning of his name.

P'u-sa is the abbreviated form of *p'u-t'i sa-va* (bodhisattva). *Pu-ti* (*bodhi*) means wisdom. *Sa-va* (*sattva*) indicates skillful means. These two benefits bestow peace and happiness on all sentient beings. *Bodhi* also means enlightenment, the fruition of wisdom. *Sattva* means sentient beings. Bodhisattvas enlighten sentient beings by means of their compassion. Because of their great vows, they are called "bodhisattvas." *Sattva* also refers to heroic diligence. Therefore, one who seeks enlightenment heroically with diligence is called a "bodhisattva." *Sattva* can also mean the practitioner, so one who seeks perfect enlightenment (*saṃbodhi*) is also called a "bodhisattva."

Kuan-tzu-tsai Bodhisattva possesses wisdom and compassion, universally practices kindness, perpetuates the pure lands, and rescues the defiled worlds. Because the potential [of the bodhisattva] and the response [of beings] are mutually related to one another, he is called "Kuan-tzu-tsai." Any being who has reached such a high level must possess great aspiration, and must have achieved profound wisdom [that] can be called "Kuan-tzu-tsai." *Kuan* refers to this apprehension. It does not necessarily refer to that bodhisattva who travels here from the Western [Pure Land], although the *Mahāprajñāpāramitā-sūtra* does not make this point clear.

SUTRA: WHEN PRACTICING THE PROFOUND *PRAJÑĀPĀRAMITĀ*,

Commentary: The Madhyamikans comment that the following passage expounds the emptiness of dharmas so as to eliminate attachment to them. The *Mahāprajñāpāramitā-sūtra* says, "*Prajñāpāramitā* is imperceptible and the name *prajñāpāramitā* is also imperceptible, because *prajñāpāramitā* is empty of inherent existence, and the name *prajñāpāramitā* is likewise empty."

The Yogācārins comment that apparently only after one has trained in wisdom can one understand the nature of emptiness; therefore, the sutra first indicates the dharmas to be practiced. The second encouragement of mind is this: when a person sees that the countless deeds of a bodhisattva are difficult to practice and begins to retrogress, he should thus encourage himself:

> "From beginningless time I have been able to endure all sorts of suffering merely in the pursuit of worldly pleasures, to say nothing of [doing so in order to] seek enlightenment. Just as in order to transcend birth and death and out of concern for the various types of unfortunate sentient beings, Kuan-tzu-tsai Bodhisattva has practiced this profound wisdom, I should do the same. I should improve self-awareness and not retrogress."

Initially, Śāriputra developed great aspiration. But because of an incident in which he gave his own eyes, he retreated to seek lesser fruition. In order to prevent him from retrogressing further, exhortation and encouragement were given.

Madhyamikans assert that conventionally speaking, practice means that in order to realize transcendent, nondiscriminating wisdom and right contemplation of emptiness, one should train to acquire that wisdom which is obtained from hearing and reflecting and which can do away with the *ālambana* (object-support). Training to develop insight into emptiness is called "practice." However, according to ultimate truth, due to the fact that there is nothing to be obtained and discriminated, there is nothing to be practiced. This, then, is what is termed "practice." The *Vimalakīrtinirdeśa-sūtra* says that non-practice is enlightenment because there should be no conceptualization. The *Mahāprajñāpāramitā-sūtra* also says, "One does not perceive practice and does not perceive non-practice because there is no inherent nature." Now, what we call "practice" is
525a actually non-practice; this is what is meant by practice. It is not that there is something to be practiced. From another perspective, in another interpretation of practice it is asserted that there is nothing to be practiced and that there is nothing that cannot be practiced. This is what is meant by practice. If there was something to be practiced and something that could not be practiced, this could not be called "practice." Again, it is explained that any conceptualization or grasping is the root of samsara (birth and death), and thus is not practice. Disciplining the mind to eradicate conceptualizations is the root of transcending worldly existence. This is practice.

The Yogācārins say that although a magician who plays tricks cannot actually transform anything, it appears that he can. Similarly, due to causes and conditions, a person hears the Dharma, believes it, trains to realize it, and teaches it without forsaking it for a moment. However, nondiscriminating, not seeing the marks of practice (*hsing-hsiang*) (i.e., the various experiential and meditative realms of cognition) is what is meant by practice. It is not that there is no need to practice. It is the "illness" [of erroneous conceptualization] that should be eliminated, not the Dharma. If there are fundamentally no dharmas that can be practiced or from which one can sever [attachment], then those ignorant of the Dharma will claim that they are already enlightened and, wrongly claiming to be enlightened, they will cause themselves great harm. Since the substance of the "flowers" [seen in the sky] due to cataracts of the eyes is empty, the flowers are not what needs to be cured. Since these flowers do not exist, how can they be eliminated? However, if the cataract is not eliminated, there will be no healthy eye. How does ultimate truth (*paramārtha*) reveal that the [sky] flower is essentially empty?

If there is nothing that is to be practiced and nothing that is not practiced, and if the unenlightened state of sentient beings is nothing other than enlightenment, then all beings should have been enlightened from beginningless time. However, from the very beginning, they are not enlightened; so, who is it that is enlightened? This is like the presumptions of non-action of the heretics, which contradict reason and violate the doctrine. How can they accomplish the wisdom of enlightenment? If terminating conceptualization were a genuine [exclusive] practice, no-thought would be the true and perfect path, all precepts would be useless, and training would be forsaken. Consider this carefully and quickly eliminate such a perverted view.

Here *practice* means that although a person practices, he does not perceive that he is practicing. This does not mean that there is no need for practice. The sutra asserts, "One does not perceive practice and does not perceive non-practice because conventionally there is practice while ultimately there is no practice." Otherwise, the sutra would have only said that one does not perceive practice. But it further states, "One does not perceive non-practice." From what is implied, the latter interpretation is correct.

The qualities of the Buddha, supreme and boundless, cannot be attained without extensive practice. Consequently a practitioner should possess the two natures (*gotra*) articulated in Mahayana

Buddhism in order to cultivate step by step the five stages of practice [leading to enlightenment]. The two natures are: (1) *Innate nature,* which means the fundamental consciousness (i.e., *ālaya-vijñana*) that is capable of producing innately all sorts of uncontaminated activities; and (2) *Acquired nature,* which is obtained through perfuming upon hearing the true Dharma. How does one know that one has an innate nature through which a person cultivates the causes of perfect enlightenment? [The way is as follows.]

One is by nature inclined to take delight in giving to, praising, and encouraging others; at the appropriate time, to advise others to engage in inoffensive deeds; not to repudiate debts nor appropriate entrusted goods; not to become attached to great wealth. Such a person has a gentle disposition and does not harm others with vicious actions. If a transgression is committed, he quickly repents and continually practices compassion. He recognizes people's kindness to him and repays their kindness. He does not breach regulations but takes delight cultivating blessings and becomes greatly alarmed about even an insignificant misdeed. Hearing of others'
525b suffering, he feels even greater pain. Identifying with goodness and repudiating evil, he never speaks harshly to inferiors and always praises and admires the virtuous. When harmed, he is not the least vindictive. Readily accepting apology, he never harbors hatred or nurses a grudge. Diligent by nature, he rises early and retires late. Being courageous and determined, he likes to do things perfectly. Being righteous, he is fearless and does not despise himself. Reflecting on the meaning of the Dharma, he ponders it carefully. He takes delight in quietude and longs to leave the household life. He does not forget whatever he does. He feels compassion even toward those with ill-will. Intelligent by nature, he accomplishes whatever he studies. Avoiding transgressions, he has the ability to discriminate [between right and wrong]. Such a nature is not capable of generating afflictions, or of creating the karma that results in unremitting suffering or that severs the roots of virtue. If born in evil destinies, he can quickly get out without having to undergo serious suffering. If he must bear a bit of suffering, this only

helps increase his disgust toward such misfortunes and deepens his compassion for suffering beings. When one recognizes that apparent characteristics such as generosity are in the majority and transgressions are in the minority, then one understands that one definitely has the innate nature of enlightenment.

However, people still abide in cyclic existence because they have not yet met truly beneficial friends to explain enlightenment to them. Even if they have [met such people], they grasp the skillful means of training erroneously, or they learn so slowly that their roots of virtue do not mature. Hence, they continue in the cycle of samsara.

After one enters the five stages [of practice leading to enlightenment], the boundless, supreme, wholesome Dharma to be practiced is called "acquired nature." What are the five paths?

1. The stage of accumulating provisions (*sambhārāvasthā*). This includes the initial aspiration to seek full enlightenment (i.e., *bodhicitta*), up to the practice of the four contemplations and the practice of the forty stages. [The forty stages are as follows:]

A. Ten aspects of *faith:* (1) faith; (2) vigor; (3) mindfulness; (4) wisdom; (5) meditation; (6) giving or non-retrogression; (7) precepts; (8) protection [of the truth]; (9) vow; and (10) transference.

B. Ten aspects of *abiding:* (1) resolution; (2) basis of discipline; (3) cultivation; (4) noble birth; (5) skillful means; (6) proper thought; (7) non-retrogression; (8) perfection as a son of the Buddha (i.e., a bodhisattva); (9) being a prince of the Dharma; and (10) initiation as in the consecration of kings.

C. Ten stages of *practice:* (1) joyful service; (2) beneficial service; (3) freedom from resentment; (4) limitlessness; (5) separation from ignorance; (6) manifestation in any form at will; (7) nonattachment; (8) exaltation; (9) wholesome dharmas; and (10) manifestation of perfect, ultimate reality.

D. Ten stages of *transference:* (1) saving and protecting sentient beings; (2) indestructible transference; (3) equaling all Buddhas; (4) omnipresence; (5) storing endless merits; (6)

pursuing roots of virtue impartially; (7) regarding all sentient beings equally; (8) following suchness; (9) not being afflicted and attached; and (10) the limitless *dharmadhātu*.

2. *The stage of intensified effort* (*prayogāvasthā*). This refers to the four kinds of meditative stabilization (*samādhi*) after the stage of accumulating provisions. [The four kinds are:] (1) the *samādhi* that achieves illumination; (2) the *samādhi* that increases illumination; (3) the *samādhi* of spontaneous recognition; and (4) continuous, unintermittent *samādhi*.

3. *The stage of penetrating understanding* (*prativedhāvasthā*). After having cultivated the four kinds of *samādhi* in the stage of intensified effort, at the entry level of the first *bhūmi* one attains the *darśana-mārga* (path of vision) in which the true characteristics of mind are first seen.

4. *The path of cultivation* (*bhāvanā-mārga*) is the ten *bhūmi*s ranging from the path of vision (*darśana-mārga)* up to the *vajra samādhi*. The ten stages of the ten *bhūmi*s are described as: (1)
525c utmost joy; (2) freedom from defilement; (3) illumination; (4) glowing wisdom; (5) difficult to conquer; (6) immediate presence; (7) proceeding far; (8) attaining calm unperturbedness; (9) finest wisdom; and (10) Dharma cloud.

5. *The stage of ultimate realization* (*niṣṭhāvasthā*). After the acquisition of the *vajra samādhi,* this is the stage of liberation which comprises the three Buddha bodies, the four kinds of perfect nirvana, and the perfect fruition of Buddhahood.

Although a person may know the five stages, how are they to be put into practice? Any practitioner who wishes to gain enlightenment and to perform deeds of great benefit should first bring forth the mind of great enlightenment (*bodhicitta*) before actually engaging in practice. Just as the first drop of water in the great ocean can be the abode of jewels, similarly this initial aspiration can be the source of the wholesome dharmas of the five vehicles. Again, just as the initial formation of the world is the source for supporting sentient beings, so this mind is the support and foundation for innumerable varieties of beings on the five paths. Again, just as the realm of space contains everything, so does the mind of great enlightenment. Since it rejects conditioned [dharmas] and partial emptiness, it realizes enlightenment as a whole and is deeply concerned with sentient beings who are as measureless as space. Although this initial aspiration might be rudimentary it can accumulate inexpressible endless blessings; how much more so can the merits derived from the motivation generated throughout successive *kalpas*.

What causes a person to generate the mind of enlightenment (*bodhicitta*)? The causes are: (1) seeing and hearing about the supernatural powers of the Buddhas; (2) hearing the teachings of bodhisattvas; (3) seeing or hearing that the Buddha-Dharma is declining and realizing that the existence of the Dharma can eliminate great suffering; and (4) seeing people in the final *kalpa* being ignorant, shameless, stingy, jealous, full of suffering, vicious, idle, and faithless, one reflects, "When such evils and afflictions exist in this troubled world, I should generate the mind of enlightenment so that others can follow my example and develop their minds of enlightenment." Due to these four causes, a person develops the great aspiration for enlightenment.

Prior to generating the mind of enlightenment, one should first be equipped with the ten supreme virtues and the three profound *vipaśyanās* (contemplations). The ten supreme virtues are: (1) being near beneficial friends; (2) making offerings to the Buddhas; (3) accumulating roots of virtue; (4) aspiring toward the supreme Dharma; (5) being kindhearted; (6) tolerating hardship; (7) being compassionate and sincere; (8) having the profound thought of equanimity; (9) believing in the Mahayana; and (10) aspiring toward the wisdom of the Buddhas.

The first of the three profound *vipaśyanās* (*kuan*) is to become weary of conditioned dharmas. This means to contemplate that in the unfortunate states of cyclic existence one is ceaselessly bombarded by suffering, that in one's body the five *skandhas* and four elements produce negative actions, that measureless afflictions inflame body and mind while the nine orifices constantly emit thirty-six types of filthy impurities, that thoughts are transient like bubbles and foam, and that ignorance produces actions which result in one's continued migration in the cycles of the six stages of existence. After carefully contemplating all these, one grows weary of the world.

The second *vipaśyanā* is to seek enlightenment. This means to contemplate the fine, magnificent characteristics of the Buddha, the original purity of the *dharmakāya,* and the powers that derive from holding precepts and supreme dharmas such as fearlessness. It means to perfect the two wonderful wisdoms through which the Buddha shows compassion for sentient beings, guides ignorant and
526a confused beings to the right path, and eradicates the afflictions that sentient beings encounter. Recognizing this accumulation of merits, one will aspire toward enlightenment.

The third *vipaśyanā* concerns sentient beings. It means to contemplate that sentient beings, who are deluded by ignorance and craving, undergo great suffering. Not believing in the law of cause and effect, they create the causes of negative actions. Forsaking the true Dharma, they trust and accept heretical doctrines. They float along with the four currents [of illusion, desire, existence, and ignorance] and are tormented by the seven afflictions. Although beings fear suffering, they continue to perform negative actions. As a result, they create misery and afflictions for themselves. Although experiencing the suffering that derives from parting from loved ones, they still indulge in attachments; although aware that meeting with what they hate causes distress, still they are full of enmity. For the sake of desire, they create karma and never tire of life's miseries. They violate precepts against [mere] pleasure, and by harboring anxieties and indulging in idleness, they perform actions resulting in the unintermittent suffering [of the hells]. Being obstinate and shameless, they denigrate the Mahayana, and their ignorance and grasping give rise to arrogance. Even if intelligent, they completely sever their virtuous roots. Being totally arrogant, they never repent. Born into the state of the eight difficulties and lacking the Dharma, they are unable to study. Although they may hear the

Dharma, they do not follow it; on the contrary, they engage in negative actions. They call worldly attainments evidence of nirvana. After indulging in worldly pleasures, they are reborn in unfortunate migrations. Seeing beings such as these, one cannot help feeling deep sorrow, and will respond by generating one's initial aspiration: "I vow to definitely realize unsurpassed, supreme enlightenment (*anuttarā-samyak-saṃbodhi*) in order to benefit all sentient beings."

One should delight in hearing the names of the Buddhas such as Śākyamuni Buddha who similarly generated this aspiration. A verse says:

> In the three immeasurable *kalpa*s,
> The Buddha Vipaśyin previously appeared [during the
> third immeasurable *kalpa*].
> Before him were Dīpaṃkara and Ratnaśikhin,
> Then in this *kalpa* Śākyamuni appeared.

The Bodhisattva Asaṅga said:

> The increasing power of purity
> And the victorious progress of a resolute mind
> Are called the first stage of bodhisattva practice
> In three immeasurable *kalpa*s.

In this first stage, a person develops faith, vigor, mindfulness, concentration, and wisdom so as to eradicate hidden defilements. Next, one generates an aspiration to meet beneficial friends of positive affinity. Even when encountering evil friends who are an obstructive and evil influence, one never forsakes the aspiration for enlightenment (*bodhicitta*). One's practice of the pure Dharma progressively improves through exhorting oneself to never falter or regress. This is known as the initial stage of practice.

By generating the initial aspiration described above, a person proceeds toward unsurpassed enlightenment and prepares to enter the Mahayana path to become a bodhisattva. The amount of time one must spend in cyclic existence is thereby limited. By continuing to progress energetically, one is assured of quickly reaching the other shore.

Next, one continues to practice. There are two categories of practice here: the abridged and extensive types. The abridged type consists of three aspects: (1) the sphere; (2) the actual practice; and (3) the results obtained. Formerly, being unable to distinguish what is true from what is illusory, one created various afflictions and therefore underwent the resultant suffering and hardship. There are three steps to reverse this trend. The first step is to carefully observe objects of cognition (*viṣaya*); then, after discerning what is right and wrong, one should stop doing
526b wrong and practice what is right. Finally, when the causal practice is perfected, the resultant virtue will be attained. Although the sacred teachings of the Buddhas are boundless, it is said that there are no more than these three categories of practice; therefore a practitioner should train accordingly.

What is meant by the object of contemplation? It means to contemplate what has arisen from conditions, namely, that all *rūpa* (forms), *citta* (mind), and *caitta*s (cognitive factors associated with mind) are like flowers in the sky and that their appearance deceives and confuses ignorant beings. This is called [the nature of] dependence on others (*paratantra*). Ignorant beings lack understanding and thus mistakenly take these things to be [real] selves and dharmas, while in actuality their nature and appearance are like flowers in the sky, nonexistent. This is called mere imagination (*parikalpita*). Both self and dharmas arise from dependent nature and are fundamentally empty. The truth that manifests through the contemplation of this emptiness is likened to [the vastness of] empty space and is called ultimate reality (*pariniṣpanna*).

All known dharmas do not spill over [into the categories of] existence, nonexistence, non-dharmas, and substantial nonexistence. Those [categories] can, in short, be called "schematizing what one attaches to" (*chui-suo-chih; parikalpita*), since what one attaches to (*suo-chih*) is what the mind perversely schematizes everywhere (*pien-chi*). One should differentiate between the existence of dharmas and substantial existence. All conditioned dharmas (*saṃskṛta-dharmas*) are called "dependent on others to arise" (*paratantra*), since phenomena (*shih; vastu*) arise from conditions. All unconditioned (*asaṃskṛta*) [dharmas] are called "consummate" since that is the fundamental principle of dharmas.

There is another interpretation which claims that contaminated (*sāsrava*) dharmas are "dependent on others to arise" (*paratantra*), because their nature is perverse (*tien-tao,* literally, "upside-down"; *viparyāsa*), while all uncontaminated (*anāsrava*) dharmas are called "consummate," since they are not perverse.

After understanding [the nature of] the field of objects of cognition (*viṣaya-gocara*), one should engage in proper practice which is perfected by (1) hearing [the Dharma], (2) contemplating [it], and (3) practicing [it]. These three kinds of practice alone encompass all virtues and wisdom. However, the most fundamental practice is the supreme consciousness only [approach], for it penetrates the most profound essence and is at once expedient, opportune, unequaled, unsurpassed, and faultless. Whether it be sudden enlightenment, gradual enlightenment, Hinayana or Mahayana, it is expounded according to this profound doctrine. The *Avataṃsaka-sūtra* says:

> The mind, like a skillful painter,
> Variously paints the five *skandha*s.
> In all the worlds
> There is nothing the mind does not create.
>
> As is the mind, so is Buddha,
> As is Buddha, so are sentient beings.
> The mind, Buddha, and sentient beings,
> All three are without distinction.
>
> All Buddhas understand that
> Everything evolves from mind.
> One who can understand likewise
> Is one who can see the truth of the Buddha.

> Body is not mind
> And mind is not body,
> Yet they give rise to all functions
> And are as free as never having been.
>
> If one wished to understand
> All Buddhas of the three periods of time,
> One should understand and contemplate
> That all Tathāgatas are created by mind.

The *Mahāprajñāpāramitā-śāstra* (*Ta-chih-tu-lun*) says:

> The bodhisattva repeatedly reflects as such, "Everything in the three realms is created by mind, for one can perceive all thoughts of the mind. Through mind one perceives the
> 526c Buddha, and through mind one becomes a Buddha. Mind is Buddha and mind is my body. The mind neither understands itself nor sees itself. If a person is attached to the appearances of the mind, he lacks wisdom and the mind is also illusory, for it arises from ignorance. Through [understanding] the appearances of the mind, one can penetrate the reality of all dharmas."

Therefore, contemplating consciousness only is foremost. "Consciousness" (*shih*) means "mind" (*hsin*). The causal mind is like a master artist that paints with dharmas. Nominally it stands alone, and yet it includes other dharmas. The word *"mātra"* ("only") is used to refute [the idea] that the grasped self and dharmas exist apart from mind. The word *"vijñāna"* ("consciousness") is used to indicate that the nature of conditioned dharmas is not apart from the mind. Consciousness only (*vijñapti-mātra*) shows that there are definitely no dharmas apart from the mind. However, this does not mean that nothing exists except the mind, because worthy and unworthy friends, causes and effects, noumena and phenomena, conventional and ultimate, are not nonexistent. The nature of "schematizing what one attaches to" (*chi suo-chih; parikalpita*) is only erroneous (*hsu-wang*) consciousness. The nature of "dependent on others to arise" (*paratantra*) is only conventional (*vyavahāra*) consciousness. The nature of the "consummate" is only ultimate (*paramārtha*) consciousness. A verse says:

> Hungry ghosts, animals, human beings, and gods,
> According to their different preceptions,
> Perceive the same thing differently.
> [One should] admit that their referent (*yi; artha*) is not a substantial reality (*chen-shih; dravya*).
>
> In regard to phenomena of the past and future,
> As in dream images or mirror reflections,
> Although the object-support (*ālambana*) is not real,
> Still the marks of objects of cognition (*viṣaya-lakṣaṇa*s) are posited.

Many sutras and *śāstra*s have repeatedly explained the principle of consciousness only, yet excessive explanations should be avoided lest the reader lose interest. Examining carefully the sacred teachings that expound the doctrine of consciousness only, we find that although there are numerous kinds, they can be categorized into five.

1. *Eradicating the false and maintaining the true.* This is to contemplate things of mere imagination (*parikalpita*) that arise from illusion as lacking substance and function. In this way one should eradicate [false perceptions]. Contemplating that all dharmas of dependent nature (*paratantra*) and true nature (*pariṇispanna*) are substantially true in the sphere of the two wisdoms, one maintains their existence. A verse says:

> One must analyze the fact that
> The interdependence of name and form is incidental.
> These two should be considered
> As merely of the mind and conventional designation.
>
> True wisdom perceives the meaning of nonexistence [of objects],

Only the three discernments [of their name, essence,
and difference].
If one sees that when [these objects] do not exist, those
discernments do not exist,
One understands the three natures.

Eradicating refers to the contemplation (*vipaśyanā*) of emptiness which eliminates grasping at existence, while *maintaining* refers to the contemplation of existence which counteracts grasping at emptiness. Contemplation on emptiness and existence eliminates [grasping at] either existence or emptiness. If there were no [grasping at] existence and emptiness, there would be no [need to contemplate] emptiness and existence. Because emptiness and existence are mutually dependent, if one contemplates only existence or only emptiness, what is emptiness and what is existence? Therefore, if one wishes to gain insight into the nature of the Dharma that transcends words, one should depend on this skillful method. This is not to say that emptiness and existence are all determined. In the stage of true *vipaśyanā*, there is neither exist-
527a ence nor emptiness because dharmas are neither discriminated nor conceptualized. To say that the truth can be realized through the contemplation of emptiness simply means that by contemplating self and dharmas grasped by mere imagination as empty, one gains insight into reality. The essence of reality is not empty. The doctrine of consciousness only teaches the counteracting of grasping; however, if one grasps at the true existence of consciousness, then that is also grasping which needs to be eliminated.

This first *vipaśyanā* applies to various doctrines explained in the sutras, such as consciousness only, the two truths, the three natures, the three nonexistences, the three emancipations, the three kinds of unproduced forbearance, the four established doctrines (*siddhārtha*), the four solemn voluntary discourses (*udāna*), the four analytical contemplations, the four true wisdoms, the five meditations on patience, and so forth. All these are included in this *vipaśyanā*.

2. *Rejecting the false and preserving the pure.* Although the noumenal and phenomenal are not separate from consciousness, objects of cognition (*viṣaya*) and mind both occur within consciousness. Mind arises necessarily by apprehending the arising of a field of objects of cognition (*viṣaya-gocara*). [The sutras] only speak of "consciousness only" not "object of cognition only," because the objects of cognition only arise within consciousness but are thought of as external. Afraid that [some] may be misled by this [apparent externality], [the sutras] only say "consciousness only." But ignorant people in their confusion grasp at dharmas, engage in afflicted actions, and are thus drawn into cyclic existence. They do not understand mental contemplation, nor do they diligently seek liberation. Out of compassion for such beings, the doctrine of consciousness only has been expounded so that they may reflect on mind and gain liberation from samsara. This is not to imply that the object of cognition within [consciousness], like the [imagined entity existing] externally, is entirely nonexistent. To prevent the overflow of the object of cognition into [erroneous notions of external] existence, it is not labeled "*mātra*" ("only"). Since the substance of the mind is pure, it is said to be consciousness only. Therefore, a sutra says,

> The object-supports (*suo-yuan; ālambana*) of mind (*citta*), thought (*manas*), and [mental] consciousness (*mano-vijñāna*) are not apart from their self-natures (*svabhāva*). Therefore, I say that everything is nothing but consciousness.

Some other sutras also say that the three realms are consciousness only. One-pointed concentration falls under this category of *vipaśyanā*.

3. *Gathering the branches (parts) into the root (foundation).* Objects of cognition (*viṣaya*) appear clearly to the mind and so does the functioning of the mind. Both [phenomena and the functioning of the mind] exist in dependence on consciousness. Apart from consciousness, there is definitely neither the foundation [i.e., the functioning of the mind] nor the parts [i.e., phenomena].

The *Triṃśikā* (*Thirty Verses*) says:

> Due to the provisional expressions (*upacāra*) "self" (*ātman*) and dharmas,
> There are a proliferation (*yu chung-chung*) of mutual operations (*pravartate*).
> They (i.e., the interactions of self and dharmas) depend on transformations of consciousness (*suo-pien*).
> That which is capable of transformation (*neng-pien*) has only three [types].

The *Ch'eng wei-shih lun* explains the theory of transformation. It says that the substance of consciousness appears in two aspects, namely, the object perceived and the perceiving faculty. They arise out of a third division called "self-apprehension." The *Saṃdhinirmocana-sūtra* says that all consciousnesses and object-supports (*so-yüan; ālambana*) are projected (*suo-hsien*) by consciousness only. The categories "objective" (*nimitta*) and "subjective" (*darśana*) are branches that return to the consciousness root. Contemplations on noumena and phenomena, the true and the conventional, etc., belong to this category of *vipaśyanā*.

4. *Concealing the inferior and revealing the superior.* Both the mind (*citta*) and its *caitta*s (mental attributes) can transform. But one says "mind only" rather than "*caitta*s only" since mind is the ruler, the one in charge. The mental attributes are inferior in that they depend on the primary mind. The inferior is covert, i.e., not apparent; only the superior is overt. Therefore, Maitreya said:

> The mind seems to appear in two aspects:
> Defiled, such as covetousness,
> Or pure, such as faith,
> And there are no defiled or pure phenomena apart from the mind.

The *Vimalakīrti*[*nirdeśa*]-*sūtra* says that whether things appear to be defiled or pure depends upon the mind. All such contemplations fall into this category of *vipaśyanā*.

5. *Eradicating forms and realizing its self-nature.* Consciousness reveals both noumena and phenomena. Phenomena are the functional aspect of noumena and should not be grasped at. Noumena is the ultimate nature and should be realized. A verse says: 527b

A rope is mistakenly perceived to be a snake.
Seeing the rope, one realizes it is not [a snake].
Realizing the actual nature of the object,
One recognizes one's mistaken perception of a snake.

Other sutras assert that the self-nature of the mind is pure. All dharmas are sacred in that they are suchness, since the characteristic of being dependent on others (*paratantra*) is the root nature of consciousness. The [sutras] also expound upon ultimate truth, the one vehicle, "single-reliance," Buddha-nature, the *dharmakāya,* the *tathāgatagarbha,* emptiness, suchness, freedom from appearances, non-production and non-cessation, nonduality, nondiscrimination, beyond language, and so forth. All these belong to this category of *vipaśyanā.*

The five categories mentioned above—emptiness and existence, the phenomenal and the mind, function and substance, mind and its attributes, noumena and phenomena—proceed from the gross to the subtle and expound progressively the profound principle of consciousness only. They include all types of *vipaśyanā* and take wonderful wisdom derived from hearing, reflecting, and practicing as the essence of *vipaśyanā.* To be able to understand clearly and discern properly is not innate or inborn. Contemplations in the desire realm (*kāmadhātu*) include only the wisdom derived from hearing and reflection. Contemplations in the form realm (*rūpadhātu*) include the wisdom obtained from hearing and practice; and contemplations in the formless realm (*arūpadhātu*) include the wisdom derived from practice only. The practice of uncontaminated *vipaśyanā* encompasses the former two contemplations.

In practicing these *vipaśyanā*s of consciousness only, beginning with the generation of the initial aspiration up through the forty stages, relying on hearing and reflecting, one deepens one's faith in the Dharma. In accordance with the circumstances encountered, one reflects on the teachings so that the contemplating mind progressively improves. In the stage of cultivation one still cannot get insight into the emptiness of the two attachments. Although one does have some practice, it is still not superior. In the stage of intensified effort, one engages in the four *vipaśyanā*s arising from the four analytical contemplations. These are to contemplate carefully that whatever one attaches to, either the terms used, the meaning, or their self-nature, exists nominally but does not really exist. By developing true knowledge in this way, one thoroughly realizes that the apprehending consciousness does not really exist. The esteemed Compassionate One (i.e., the Buddha) taught this in the following verse:

> A bodhisattva, in the state of *samādhi,*
> Perceives that images are merely the mind.
> Having eradicated discursive thoughts,
> He realizes that there is merely his own projection.
>
> Abiding within the mind this way,
> One knows that what is grasped does not exist,
> Nor does that which grasps (i.e., the grasper).
> Subsequently, nothing is sensed (*sparśa*).

A bodhisattva in this stage is able to practice *vipaśyanā* but still clings to appearance and therefore cannot realize truth. In the stage of penetrating understanding, nothing whatsoever is attained amid *ālambana*s and *viṣaya*s by nondiscriminating wisdom. When principle and cognition (*chih; jñāna*) are conjoined, mind and objects of cognition (*viṣaya*s) profoundly encounter [each other]. When the marks of existence and emptiness are not immediately present (*hsien-ch'ien*), the true principle of consciousness only is said to be realized and attained. A root verse says:

> If, when [perceiving] an object-support (*ālambana*),
> Nothing whatsoever is attained by cognition,

At that same moment one is abiding in consciousness only
Since there is no mark of grasped (*grāhya*) nor grasper
(*grāhaka*). 527c

After realizing ultimate truth and acquiring the wisdom of subsequent attainment (*pṛṣṭhalabdha-jñāna*), conventional cognition is realized. The *Ho-yen ching* (*Great Adornment Sutra*) says:

It's not that one doesn't see suchness,
And yet is able to understand the practices.
They are like magical occurrences,
Although existent, they are unreal (i.e., not what they seem).

In this stage, a bodhisattva comprehends the *dharmadhātu,* abides in the [first] *bhūmi* of utmost joy, is born into the family of the Tathāgata, and is aware that supreme enlightenment is soon to be attained. In the stage of practice, there are different degrees of practice. In the first four *bhūmis*, the ultimate and the conventional meanings of consciousness only are realized separately. In the fifth *bhūmi,* the two are to some extent contemplated jointly; however, even the bodhisattva who is extremely diligent cannot achieve this constantly and effortlessly. In the seventh *bhūmi,* although contemplation on consciousness as true and conventional can be maintained for a long time, one still requires further practice. Beyond the eighth *bhūmi,* one practices effortlessly, spontaneously, and naturally in the domain of emptiness, giving rise to superior practices. In the stage of complete realization, one requires no further practice—every thought is capable of [producing cognitive] conditions (*neng-yuan; ālambaka*) of ultimate or conventional consciousness.

Two things are to be worked on during practice. They are (1) what is presented to cognition, and (2) hidden latencies, or seeds (*bījas*). In the first two stages, the three wisdoms (hearing, thinking, and cultivation), in terms of the two practices (cognitive presentation and seeds [*bījas*]), are understood to be contaminated (*sāsrava*), while the seeds being cultivated are uncontaminated (*anāsrava*). In the stage of penetrating understanding, one uncontaminatedly cultivates the [three] wisdoms. As to presentation and seeds, in [this stage of] practice, only the seeds are understood to be contaminated. In the stage of cultivation, prior to the seventh *bhūmi,* the three wisdoms are both contaminated *(sāsrava)* and uncontaminated (*anāsrava*). As to presentation and seeds, in this stage of practice, above the eighth *bhūmi* only seeds are contaminated; the three wisdoms are uncontaminated. As to presentation and seeds in the final stage, they are all understood to be contaminated, and [thus] are all eliminated. Although [all that subsequently remains] is uncontaminated, both presentation and seeds are said to be cultivated. One must contemplate the unfolding of seeds and presentation, increasingly perfecting them until perfected.

Practice here means to contemplate the fact that manifest activities and potentialities mutually intensify and develop until perfected. Those who have gained mastery, even in the lower stages, are capable of higher practices, while those who have not gained mastery are not. The practice of consciousness only encompasses all other practices, because all [other practices] depend upon the practice of consciousness only.

In short, what results are to be obtained by practice? Contaminated practices are able to produce all sorts of wondrous results in the world [enmeshed in] fictitious mental elaborations (*prapañca*), while uncontaminated practices eliminate forever all obstructions, [lead to] attaining great *bodhi,* and benefit all beings until the end of time. This is to explain them separately, but when the two practices are conjoined, they are all-encompassing.

The above explanation is a brief presentation of practice. What is the expanded exposition of practice? It consists of three aspects: (1) what is taught; (2) the [dharma] of cultivating the teachings; and (3) the one able to cultivate the teachings. First of all, one should know what is taught, one should rely on that teaching, and, finally, one methodically accomplishes what he is able to cultivate from the teachings. Thus, all three aspects are included in the bodhisattva practice.

The first aspect, the object of practice, includes five things:

1. *Regarding those to be trained.* One should clearly recognize that people differ by *gotra* (i.e., "family" type determined by inherent seeds), namely, those belonging to the three vehicles, those of undetermined nature, and *icchantika*s (beings lacking the pure seeds of enlightenment), and each ripens according to their own capabilities.

2. *Regarding beneficial deeds.* These include deeds benefiting oneself, such as seeking wealth for personal pleasure, seeking the Dharma but holding to it selfishly, taking delight in holding precepts for the purpose of birth in the heavens, making offerings to the Three Jewels with an impure aim, boasting of one's own merits for fame and gain, freeing others from difficulties in order to 528a
create allies, and being attached to the pleasure of meditation without thought of benefiting other sentient beings. If one wishes to engage in deeds purely benefiting others, deeds such as practicing generosity with deviant views, teaching the Dharma without the view of causality, or teaching without practicing oneself should all be totally abandoned. And the two faultless benefits should be diligently practiced.

3. *Regarding true meaning.* True suchness that sees things as they are, the perception of all phenomena whatsoever, the realization of the mundane, the realization of doctrinal principles, and the wisdom resulting from the purification of the two obstructions (i.e., of the known [*jñeyāvaraṇa*] and of the afflictions [*kleśāvaraṇa*]) should be cultivated and [the two obstructions] should be eradicated.

4. *Regarding power.* The supernatural powers, from those derived from the six perfections, such as the eradication of miserliness and so on, up to the powers resulting from good deeds that are achieved after the attainment of enlightenment. To benefit sentient beings [the Buddha] endures great suffering. He manifests the four kinds of birth as well as the eight aspects of a Buddha's life, and even unfortunate births or blindness, in order to benefit beings. From these practices the Buddha creates his power, through which he knows the circumstances, the timing, and the suitability of all beings within the *dharmadhātu*. He has the common and

uncommon supernatural powers of spiritual penetration into boundless worlds. When one knows there are such powers, one should practice diligently so as to realize Buddhahood.

5. *Regarding bodhi.* The wisdoms, abandonments, and so on, all the Buddha qualities, should be understood and engaged in extensively so as to realize the fruition of [Buddhahood].

Regarding these five aspects, one should first understand the capabilities of the beings to be taught and then begin practices to benefit them. Next, one should know what is to be practiced and what is to be eliminated, and then one benefits oneself through attaining great powers. Finally, one should vigorously and sincerely work for the realization of the final fruition of unsurpassed enlightenment.

After understanding the object of practice, one should engage in practice. The practice of the Dharma starts from attaining the benefits from the virtues of the Three Jewels, the powers of the Buddhas and bodhisattvas, and the true meaning of the infallible [law of] cause and effect. After attaining skillful means, one purely believes, comprehends, and surely delights in the excellent words of the sutras. Next, one should seek the Dharma, including all of the [five fields of knowledge (*pañca-vidyā*):] inner thought or philosophy (*adhyātma-vidyā*) of the Buddha-Dharma, logic (*hetu-vidyā*), grammar (*śabda-vidyā*), medicine (*cikitsā-vidyā*), and arts and mathematics (*śilpākarma-sthāna-vidyā*). All these should be diligently pursued.

How does one pursue them? As for inner thought, one should vigorously and enthusiastically seek to hear [the Buddha-Dharma]. Just to hear a single phrase of the excellent Dharma, one would happily walk on a road as crude as iron, let alone do so to hear many good teachings. Although oneself and one's possessions are cherished, the true Dharma [should be] cherished incomparably more. Unsatiated, tireless, with deep faith and a pure heart, and possessing right views, one cherishes virtues and the Dharma. When visiting Dharma masters, without thought of confrontation one regards them as wonderful gems, the eyes of wisdom, the light of knowledge, victors, stainless and delightful. Deeply respectful and without arrogance, one does not view them as transgressors of precepts, of low caste, ugly, unlettered, despicable, or heretical.

It is in order to seek goodness, not for displaying one's own merits nor for fame and gain, that one pursues the true Dharma. One should always respectfully listen to the teachings without belittling or finding fault [in them] nor underestimating or belittling oneself. 528b
It is for the purpose of comprehension that one gives his undivided attention.

What is the purpose of seeking [to master the five fields of knowledge]? Inner study means to continuously cultivate for one's own benefit and for awakening others. Logic is studied in order to refute heretical systems of thought and to uphold the proper path. Grammar is studied in order to induce faith and delight [in the Buddha's teaching] through expository language so that sentient beings will generate deep reverence [for it]. Medicine is studied in order to cure illnesses so that sentient beings may live healthy, happy lives. The arts are studied so that with little effort a great accumulation of precious riches may greatly benefit countless beings. One should diligently pursue these five fields of knowledge so that unobstructed wisdom may arise and one's resources may be quickly and fully accumulated.

Next, one should propagate the true Dharma and teach the five fields of knowledge in a way that is beneficial and pleasing. How should one teach? One should teach calmly in accordance with the Dharma and with dignified deportment. One should not expound the true Dharma to those who are not sick yet sit upon a high seat, because the teachings of the Buddhas and bodhisattvas are worthy of respect, and people should be taught to respect the precious treasure of the Dharma. One should teach [the Dharma] ceaselessly, withholding nothing. According to the disposition of [those one is teaching], one should explain things in sequence without thought of miserliness. This is called teaching in accordance with what is favorable. To those who hold grudges, one should maintain a compassionate attitude; to those who act negatively, one should maintain a beneficial attitude; and to those who become lax in favorable circumstances and become negative when in difficulty, one should maintain an attitude of both benefit and compassion. Without giving rise to jealousy, one should refrain from praising oneself or blaming others. Neither should one teach the Dharma for the sake of obtaining fame, gain, respect, or praise.

Next, one should engage in practice, avoiding the three types of negative actions, that is, of body, speech, and mind, as proscribed by the Buddha. Having heard teachings on positive actions, one contemplates and practices them properly. Living alone in guarded tranquility, one ponders the teachings of the Dharma one has heard. Uninterruptedly and earnestly, one contemplates and analyzes their proper significance. One seeks to understand what is not yet understood and never forgets what is already understood. What is not yet intelligible is due to one's own lack of enlightenment; therefore, one refrains from condemning or slandering the Buddha. Awed by one's own lack of wisdom, one develops strong faith with an upright mind. Knowing the profound meaning [of the Dharma] well, one is unmoved by different teachings. One concentrates one's mind beyond the realm of language, and keeps away from meaningless argumentation (*prapañca*) and disturbing thoughts. One practices calm abiding (*śamatha*) and special insight (*vipaśyanā*).

Next, one should teach. One should take into consideration the mental capacities and inclination of others. Accordingly, one should determine the practices appropriate for each, so as to cause them to forsake their arrogance and pride.

Next, one should give instructions and admonitions, forbidding offenses and explaining allowable non-offenses. As for those who have actually transgressed, temporary offenders are admonished and encouraged in accordance with the Dharma, whereas frequent offenders are either admonished or expelled according to the precepts, without malice and with a steady and beneficial attitude. Less serious offenders are suspended temporarily, while serious offenders are expelled permanently so that the offenders will not reap further misfortune. Those who are able to practice properly are praised kindly, with parables humbly explained to enhance their joyful practice.

Next, one establishes the three actions of body, speech, and mind. First, one benefits others through gifts of material wealth that induce them to listen to the teachings and, therefore, to practice. With those who are ignorant, it is appropriate to use endearing words in order that they accept and respect right principles, extricating them from transgressions and exhorting them to abide in virtue. One should work together with them in proper practice, so that they will not be inclined to say [that the teacher does not practice]. Next, one should practice the [six] perfections (*pāramitās*). 528c

The Perfection of Giving

The perfection of giving (*dāna*) is to give up position and greed with regard to the three actions. When practicing giving, one should not give things that lead only to sensual pleasure but not to virtuous benefit, or give things that lead neither to pleasure nor virtuous benefit; in other words, one should give things that lead to virtuous benefit and not pleasure, or give things that result in both virtuous benefit and pleasure. If people request material goods, one should seek to satisfy [their requests]. If they request more than [what is] necessary, then, depending on the situation, one should exhort them to eliminate their afflictions and generate contentment.

One should not give certain objects or give under certain circumstances. For example, if someone wants a knife to harm himself or others, one should not give it. [One should not give] what is not one's own possession, food containing insects, instruments of meaningless pleasure, things that kill or harm beings, or things to be used in evil sacrificial rites in such places as in water or on land where living creatures are injured or slaughtered, and where grudges and hatred accumulate. One should not give to those who frequently seek [to satisfy] their gluttonous appetites, nor help those in distress with plans to harm themselves. One should not seize things from inferiors, nor should one take delight in doing evil or seek for position. One should not rob in order to give to others, nor give away things in a violent or harmful manner, nor give something which violates one's own precepts. One should not discriminate between enemies and friends, nor give inferior things when one has promised superior things, nor give less when one has promised more. One should not give while harboring malice or enmity. Having practiced generosity, one should not publicize or boast, expecting favor in return. One should not throw or give gifts in a rude manner. If people come [to make requests] with negative minds and bad manners and one gives indiscriminately to them, one should not regard this giving as purely virtuous.

One should not practice giving simply because one is coerced by others, or out of fear of poverty [in future lives]. One should not give leftovers or dirty food to monks; nor give stolen goods or goods that have been appropriated without the owner's permission; nor give things that are not in accordance with the precepts. One should not give only after many requests and a display of subservience [from the receiver], nor give in the hope of worldly fame or of gaining favors in return. One should not give for the purpose of gaining others' respect, nor give with a narrow-minded attitude. One should not deceitfully give something small then later impoverish the person. One should not give in order to stir up ill will between two parties in order to gain their submission. One should not be lax in the practice of giving while encouraging others to give. Once should not give unequally, out of sequence, unwillingly, unhappily, or regretfully. One should not give fake things when asked for real ones. One should not ridicule those who seek help at an improper time, without forethought, or in an improper manner, causing them to feel ashamed. One should not remain silent nor refuse to give when entreated repeatedly. One should not give Buddhist teachings to outsiders whose purpose is to find fault in them, nor to those who seek the teachings for material gain and try to impress others with these teachings even though they have no real understanding of them.

The above-mentioned are faults and should all be avoided. One should do whatever is the reverse. If one does not possess sufficient wealth, one should consider if those who come for help are content and not poor, or miserable and helpless. Then, according to one's wealth, one satisfies their needs.

Those with little should delight in giving whatever they can to create contentment and happiness for whoever comes asking. If one sees a stingy person, or a person who was previously poor but hopes to create blessings, one should encourage the person to cultivate blessings and expediently guide and advise him in the following way:

> "Without loss of expense, you can still benefit others liberally. I have valuables and wealth that I will allow you to give away as you choose. Be careful not to let those who come for help return empty-handed. When I benefit them, you should accord with that virtue to cause delight in others. The seeds thus sown will gradually grow."

Seeing people come to ask for things, one should give happily. If they are deceitful and cunning and take advantage, or cheat when begging, [one should] conceal their mistakes without hurting them and fulfill their wishes. One should not disgrace or shame them, so that they can leave happily. At first they may take advantage and cheat, but sooner or later they will come to understand. Neither commend nor reproach, but rather develop pity and sympathy for them. Think: "They misunderstood me and happened to make a
mistake or fault. I will maintain a cheerful attitude and keep them 529a
from negativity." If one has no wealth or valuables to give, one should give the Dharma and sutras so that one will not fail in granting requests. One should very skillfully propagate the proper Buddha-Dharma and cause beings to learn the practice of giving. If one sees someone who often gives alms, one should have others do

likewise, so that by encouraging them to give they can attain the perfection of giving. One should not cause others to give too little, or to give improperly, or to give partially to friends, or to make offerings thoughtlessly.

Having understood the scriptures, one should copy and disseminate them for propagation. If there are no extra copies and one has no ability to copy them, one should reflect, "Am I hindered by miserliness, or am I withholding them for better use?" If hindered by miserliness, one should encourage oneself to give. One should practice giving [copies of scriptures] without miserliness even if one should become ignorant, let alone merely become short of provisions for acquiring wisdom.

If one is free of miserliness and if it is for the purpose of a better use [that one withholds scriptures], one should then reflect: "When I give [away scriptures], is it to eradicate afflictions for myself, or for sentient beings, or for perfecting wisdom?" One observes that it is not in order to eliminate one's own afflictions but in order to increase one's wealth of knowledge and enhance skillful means and wisdom, not only out of loving kindness for that person but for all other beings as well. In such cases, not giving [scriptures] does not violate pure precepts. One then skillfully explains [why one cannot give], and dismisses the person.

If one has accumulated wealth, one should offer it to the Buddhas and bodhisattvas in order to purify one's intentions. Thus, even if one accumulates wealth, one still abides in the sacred lineage. One should constantly be mindful of these blessings, increasing and extending them as if they had been entrusted to one by the Buddhas and bodhisattvas.

If one reflects that in a particular instance giving a scripture is inappropriate, one should say: "Worthy one, this is someone else's possession and cannot be given to you." One consoles [the person] with this explanation and dismisses them. Or one may take another possession [instead of a scripture] and respectfully offer it to counter the person's assumption that one is being stingy, or to explain that the scripture is not one's own property. To those with feelings of bitter enmity or virtuous benevolence, one should give with kindness, compassion, joy, and equanimity. If one encounters the four types of obstacles so that one is unable to give graciously, one should apply the four types of wisdom to counteract them:

1. If one has wealth but does not enjoy giving, one should consider that this [stinginess] results from the habits accumulated in successive past [lifetimes], and that unless one forces oneself to give, the problem will further intensify in the future. Thus, one earnestly encourages oneself in the practice and develops the wisdom of awareness.

2. If one has an attitude of not giving joyfully due to a lack of possessions, one should reflect on the causes of this lack of wealth that prevents one from giving, and summon forth an attitude of benevolence to endure the suffering of poverty. Perceiving the benefits of giving, one develops the wisdom of forbearing suffering.

3. If one takes delight in one's wealth and does not give joyfully, one should reflect that one's apparent indulgence is deceptive and foolish and will be one's downfall, and realize that it will be the source of suffering in the future. Thus, one earnestly encourages oneself to give and develops the wisdom of eradicating errors (*viparyāsa*).

4. Even if one does practice giving but does so only for worldly rewards, one should quickly and thoroughly understand that this is an erroneous view. One should contemplate that all things are impermanent, are bound to disintegrate, and will soon come to an end. Thus, one will not take delight in worldly pleasures but will certainly seek enlightenment and gain insight into impermanence.

One should abide in tranquil seclusion, summoning deep faith and continually concentrating on the thought of giving many and excellent things. Because of this intention, one can give wealth to all sentient beings. Therefore, with little effort, one can create immeasurable blessings and give away things that one treasures
and loves. One should not be miserly with what has been gained 529b
through hardship and difficulty. With faith and respect, one should graciously give in person, at the right time, and without harming oneself or others.

There are three kinds of giving. To give pure and excellent possessions extensively is the giving of wealth. To banish people's fear is the giving of fearlessness. And to exhort others to practice good deeds is the giving of the Dharma. One gives readily and does not create delays or withhold anything, though it is not because people demand things quickly that one does so. One promptly gives whatever one has, not waiting [to give] until one accumulates a lot of wealth. One should be humble with supplicants and without competitiveness or arrogance.

The Perfection of Morality

Morality (*śīla*) means receiving and studying pure actions with regard to the three actions [of body, speech, and mind]. One who practices morality purely [should have four qualities, which are to:] (1) receive the precepts properly; (2) keep them with pure intention; (3) avoid transgressions and restore the precepts purely and respectfully after violation [of them]; and (4) mindfully not transgress again. If one violates the precepts that one has properly received, one should see this as a source of shame. If one violates the pure intention [to keep the precepts], one should develop a sense of shame. Therefore, one is able to safeguard the precepts and restore them purely with respect and mindfulness. Due to the first two [of the four qualities] one can consequently avoid all negative actions. Due to the first two and the last [of these four qualities], one is able to avoid violating the precepts. If one can regain purity [through repentance] after violation, one can quickly restore [the precepts], leaving transgressions behind. Excellent and immeasurably abundant benefits are the great advantages resulting from pure morality.

Both ordained [people] and laypeople should practice the three types of morality. First is the morality of discipline. This refers to the precepts followed by the seven groups of Buddhists (i.e., *bhikṣu*s and *bhikṣuṇī*s; *śikṣamāṇā*s; *śrāmaṇera*s and *śrāmaṇerikā*s; *upāsaka*s and *upāsikā*s). Ordained Buddhists renounce even the position of a universal monarch (*cakravartin*), abandoning it happily as if it were a weed. They have no desire for divine pleasures, much less worldly wealth and position. They reject superior attainments, let alone inferior things. They vigorously engage in other practices, not being satisfied only with the practice of morality. They abandon negative speech and thought. If these arise, they quickly repent and purify them, so as to restrain their speech and collect their thoughts properly. Hearing about difficult practices, they are neither alarmed nor intimidated but apply themselves and persevere in the practice. They do not look for faults in others, but continually examine their own shortcomings. Seeing wicked and violent beings, they compassionately accept them. When harmed or offended [by someone], they neither get angry nor reject them. If they commit a violation, they repent and pledge not to transgress again. Having few desires, being happy and content, they are able to endure all suffering and are neither restless nor irritable. They are dignified in deportment, serene, and tranquil. They eschew deceit and all such negative behavior.

Second is the morality that consists of positive actions. This refers to all positive actions that are causes [for the attainment] of great enlightenment accumulated after receiving precepts. Following the precepts and abiding in solitude, one engages in hearing, *vipaśyanā,* and practice. One honors one's elders and respectfully serves the sick with mercy and compassion. One praises the goodness of others and extols those who are virtuous, rejoices in good deeds, and dedicates all merits. One vows to make offerings [to the Three Jewels] and to keep the precepts scrupulously. One is self-restrained in taking food and strictly guards the senses. During the first and last parts of the night, one continually maintains mindful alertness. One stays near virtuous beneficial friends, without much concern for one's physical body or possessions. One has no tolerance for negative actions, understands well the law of cause and effect, and also eradicates obstacles. Thus, one is able gradually and progressively to abide in the ten perfections (i.e., the six perfections of giving, morality, patience, effort, concentration, and wisdom described here, plus skillful means [*upāya*], vows [*praṇidhāna*], powers [*bala*], and knowledge [*jñāna*]).

Third is the morality of wishing to greatly benefit sentient beings. One works to help those of various inclinations in all unmistaken actions. One serves the sick, guides the blind, communicates with gestures to the deaf, explains with symbols to the mute, shows a [convenient] path to those who have gone astray, offers a resting place to the weary, provides conveyances to benefit those who are lame, and instructs the ignorant with surpassing wisdom to eradicate their hindrances. One consoles those who are despised, urging them to eliminate miserliness and negativity. One teaches how to gain wealth, arousing faith in the sacred teachings that put an end to the afflictions and remove suffering. One
529c remembers favors received, repays kindnesses, and praises and welcomes people one meets. With cheerful hospitality, one converses cordially and arranges places for [guests] to sit. One reciprocates with something of equal or greater value, not of less value.

One protects beings from fear and consoles those in sorrow. One always has wealth on hand to give away when requested. First one serves by helping people in need and then benefits them materially. If one lacks possessions, one goes searching for things to give away. One shares whatever one has and does not hoard things for oneself. One practices sincerely in accordance with what one teaches. Except for unbeneficial actions, one acts in accordance with the behavior of others. Except for censuring reprehensible transgressions, one does not annoy others nor denigrate, embarrass, or humiliate them. One does not make known others' shortcomings, nor praise oneself highly. One stays neither too close to nor too distant from people, nor does one stay near them at improper times. One does not destroy what others are fond of nor praise what they detest. One does not give out valuable information [about a matter] to those who are not closely involved [in it]. One does not make frequent or unusual requests nor revoke previous promises. All of these are part of the treasure of immeasurably great virtues.

If a bodhisattva has already developed the great aspiration to attain enlightenment and wishes to practice diligently, he should receive the [bodhisattva] precepts properly from a person who is qualified to confer them. Then this [qualified] bodhisattva will cause those who take the precepts to generate great sincerity and deep concentration so that the precepts may be properly conferred. If there is no one to give the precepts, one can take them properly oneself before an image of the Buddha. After doing this, one should constantly be mindful of the bodhisattva precepts. As to that which is proscribed, one should discern by learning, analyzing, and interpreting in accordance with the original sutras. One should not take precepts from those who extensively slander the bodhisattva texts, even though [such people] may be clever, wise, and eloquent.

One should not bestow precepts on those without faith in them, or on those who slander or denigrate them. If one maintains pure morality and is replete with great virtue, such condemnation and slander merely become great offenses for that person. If one hears [any slander from others], one should not forsake them.

One receives [precepts] not because one is urged to nor in order to outdo others, but because one chooses to do so through one's own wise judgment and firm resolve. There are four methods of trying to outdo others: (1) praising oneself and slandering others for fame, gain, and respect; (2) being miserly and not giving to those who seek wealth or the Dharma; (3) retaliating with anger, [causing] injury, and not relinquishing grudges; and (4) slandering the bodhisattva texts and happily proclaiming teachings resembling [the real teachings] that oneself believes in or that are followed by others. Committing such offenses, one is unable to increase one's pure motivation or accumulate great rewards. One is only the semblance of a bodhisattva, not a true one.

There are two causes or conditions by which a bodhisattva loses the pure [bodhisattva] precepts: (1) forsaking the great vow to attain unsurpassed enlightenment and (2) committing the most serious offense of the four *pārājika*s (i.e., offenses that are cause for expulsion from the order). Those who commit lesser or middling offenses do not lose the pure precepts. Only those who frequently, shamelessly, and happily commit the four *pārājikas* are designated the most serious offenders. Committing only one passing offense is not considered forsaking [the precepts]. Without the two conditions [mentioned above], the bodhisattva does not lose the pure precepts even in future lives. In future lifetimes, although he may forget [the precepts taken in previous lives] and receive the precepts again, it is not a new ordination but an awakening of awareness, a remembrance of them.

One who maintains the [bodhisattva] precepts should make offerings daily to the Buddha, Dharma, and Sangha (i.e., the Three Jewels), and their residences, prostrate respectfully, recite a *gāthā* (verse) of praise, generate sincere faith, and contemplate their true virtues. One should not waste any opportunity for reverence, offerings, and diligence. One should not give rise to great desire
530a but should abandon fame and gain.

One respects and serves virtuous elders, obeying them with proper manners and gratitude. One accepts proper invitations and uncontaminated offerings and gives the undefiled Dharma. One equally guards against the major and minor transgressions, and is ready to do whatever is necessary to benefit others. One maintains right livelihood and keeps the three actions [of body, speech, and mind] peacefully and harmoniously. Having revulsion for samsara, one longs for nirvana. One should defend oneself against malicious gossip or praise. One should apologize for offending others and shuld not retaliate for insults. One should discipline [one's] disciples without defiled thought. One takes the proper amount of rest at the proper time and avoids joking and chatting. One humbly seeks teachings to break through the five obstructions (*pañca-nīvaraṇa*) (i.e., sensual desire; ill will; sloth and torpor; restlessness and worry; and doubt), and does not slander the two vehicles. After thoroughly studying the bodhisattva texts, one then studies the *śrāvaka* texts. Having mastered the Buddha-Dharma, one then learns the non-Buddhist systems. Those who are highly intelligent spend two-thirds of their daily time on Buddhist studies and one-third on non-Buddhist studies, approaching the [latter] as if they had a bitter taste. Only with strong faith and love for the Dharma can one use it to bring benefit and happiness to others. When the true Dharma is being expounded, one enthusiastically goes to listen. One skillfully follows the meaning of the texts and shows great respect for Dharma masters, or even manifests supernatural powers to properly attract and lead beings. If one is insane, is oppressed by great suffering, has not taken the pure precepts, or [already] abides in the tenth *bhūmi,* then one does not make any transgressions [even if not practicing as described above]. Otherwise, one should be aware that disregarding any of the abovementioned [practices] constitutes a transgression.

If one commits a very serious transgression, one should confess before three or more masters who know the precepts well, and after confessing [one should] take the precepts again. One who commits a lesser or middling transgression may disclose it to one master. If there is no one to whom one can reveal [the transgression, one should confess] by oneself with a pure motivation, pledging not to commit the transgression again. Thus one can leave transgressions behind and restore [the precepts] to purity.

Practicing in this way, one attains three perfections: (1) the perfection of practice, meaning that by avoiding transgressions the three actions [of body, speech, and mind] are purified; (2) the perfection of thought, meaning that one leaves the household life in order to seek great enlightenment, not in order to achieve some future result; and (3) the perfection of cause, meaning that because of previous excellent actions one now attains the supreme result and is able to again practice virtue. Is this not joy and peace? Unless one learns these three, one will encounter only decline, harm, danger, and suffering.

If one abandons great wealth and position in order to keep pure precepts, avoids the slightest transgression until the end of one's life, and never becomes lax nor falls into error, one will inevitably obtain these five benefits life after life: (1) one will be protected by the Buddhas of the ten directions; (2) one will experience great joy at the time of death; (3) one will always associate with people who keep precepts; (4) one will achieve the perfection of merits; and (5) one will obtain precepts in successive lifetimes, and these precepts will perfect one's character. In order to stabilize one's mind, gain understanding of the Buddha-Dharma, and benefit beings, one mindfully avoids transgressions.

The Perfection of Patience

Patience (*kṣānti*) means to avoid anger under any circumstances, through vigorously exercising discerning wisdom. There are three kinds of patience.

1. *The patience of enduring enmity and harm.* When encountering harm from others, one should reflect:

> "This is due to my actions in previous lifetimes. If I am not patient now, I will again create the causes of suffering. Instead of benefiting myself, I will only achieve fetters and harm for myself. Moreover, both my body and mind and those of others are of the nature of suffering. Out of ignorance, others harm me physically. But as I am aware [of the consequences], how could I then increase their suffering? *Śrāvaka*s, who work for their own benefit, still do not harm others [in retaliation]. Even more so should I, working to benefit
> 530b others, endure their harm [without retaliation]."

Reflecting in this way, one should practice the *five contemplations* (*hsiang*). First is to reflect thus:

> "Since beginningless time, beings have been either my relatives or friends, so I should abandon enmity and harm and constantly remember their kindness."

Second, one should reflect:

> "Since all phenomena are dependently arising and selfless, who is there to be harmed? Hence, I should not take [enmity] personally but should maintain thoughts of the Dharma."

Third, one should reflect:

> "The nature of life is impermanent. Out of revenge I can do nothing more than end someone's life. Why would an intelligent person want to kill those who are already in the process of birth and death? I should not even allow defiled thoughts to arise, much less cause harm. I should abandon thoughts of permanence and maintain mindfulness of impermanence."

Fourth, one should reflect:

> "Whether experiencing prosperity or hardship, beings are constantly pursued by the three kinds of suffering. I should employ skillful means to lead them out of suffering forever. How could I cause them more suffering? I should abandon thoughts of pleasure and maintain mindfulness of suffering."

Fifth, one should reflect:

> "It is for the sake of sentient beings that I aspire toward enlightenment. I should benefit them and look after them. How could I retaliate and harm them? I should abandon thoughts of harming them and maintain thoughts of looking after them."

Thus, one will be free from anger, will not reciprocate harm and injury nor be led by one's predispositions, and will be able to tolerate enmity and harm.

2. *The patience of enduring suffering:* If one encounters suffering, one should think:

> "Since beginningless time, due to ignorance and faults, I have undergone much suffering in order to seek pleasure, much more than [I have endured] in pursuit of enlightenment and accomplishing the great task. Even if I have to go through great suffering for hundreds of thousands of *kalpa*s, I should accept it patiently, let alone [accept] a small amount of suffering."

One should not become distressed and angry when lacking the four necessities [of a monk] (i.e., food, clothing, a sleeping place, and medicine) or when insulted. One should endure the suffering incurred in the mundane processes of decay, destruction, sickness, and death, as well as the suffering encountered in maintaining the four types of dignified deportment, in assimilating the Dharma, in changing one's appearance (i.e., becoming ordained), in wearing cast-off clothes, in coping with self-apprehension, in going for alms, in renouncing inappropriate possessions, in abstaining from sexual pleasure, in practicing virtues, in benefiting beings, in following the Dharma, and in exerting diligence. One should be able to endure all of these patiently. One should skillfully improve and not be negligent in the pursuit of great enlightenment but eradicate the defilements of the mind without retrogressing.

3. *The patience of true insight into the Dharma.* This means to familiarize oneself with all aspects of the Three Jewels and to gain pure understanding and benevolence through analysis. One should be sympathetic with negative and lowly beings, with subordinates and enemies as well as close ones, when training oneself in the three actions both when in public and in private, day and night, and also when ill. Due to having patience toward harm and offenses, one is freed from them; and, due to patience, one can practice giving when help is sought. One benefits others constantly and abundantly without discrimination both now and in the future, not benefiting others only sporadically. One readily apologizes for offending [others] and accepts apologies for offenses, so that people will not dislike one. One becomes mortified upon losing patience and realizes that patience is the cause of peace and happiness in life. [Patience] eradicates nonvirtuous actions, leads to peace and happiness, and allows one to approach the end of one's life without regret. It leads to excellent future rebirths without hatred or enemies, and eventually to the realization of unsurpassed enlightenment. One also sees
530c the suffering that results from impatience. Therefore, one practices patience oneself, and through praise and encouragement teaches others to do the same.

The Perfection of Effort

Effort (*vīrya*) means to make courageous efforts in the practice of virtue in regard to the three actions. In brief, these are of three types:

1. *Increasing effort.* This means that before the practice of virtue, one generates a courageous attitude and dons the armor of this pledge:

> "Now, in order to liberate even one being from suffering, I am willing to stay in the hells, even though one day and night [in hell] is equal to a thousand great *kalpa*s here. If I have to stay in the hells hundreds of thousands of times before I attain enlightenment, I will do so without regret or becoming discouraged, [much less] stay for a short time and undergo [only] a little suffering."

If one can summon even a little faith and understanding [of this practice], one creates innumerable causes for the attainment of great enlightenment; how much more so if one perfects [the practice]? Therefore, one practices virtue without the least cowardice.

2. *Effort in accumulating merits.* This means that by summoning one's capabilities, one is able to perfect all practices. One should remain unmoved when facing all kinds of problems, different viewpoints, suffering, and annoyances. One should endeavor strenuously and also practice without arrogance. The World-honored One always acclaimed the practice of effort, for it enables one to perfect goodness and to actualize enlightenment quickly.

3. *Effort benefiting sentient beings.* This refers to the various efforts to benefit sentient beings as previously mentioned. One should shun thoughts of one's own physical body, wealth, and so on. Accomplishing all practices equally without interruption or laxity, one can achieve equality and understanding and accord with virtue. Practicing properly without sloth and haste, one can eliminate defilements and produce many new good deeds. The three actions [of body, speech, and mind] will be purified and the three

ways [of obtaining wisdom from hearing, reflection, and practice] will increase. One should have strength, diligence, and courage to boldly and steadily create virtue without violating good norms. One should practice vigorously, happily, and tirelessly. One should destroy afflictions as quickly as if one were extinguishing a fire on one's own head. Following the Dharma and applying it, one can protect oneself and benefit others.

The Perfection of Concentration

Concentration (*dhyāna*) means first hearing and reflecting on [the Dharma] and then stabilizing the mind one-pointedly. There are three types of concentration. First is tranquil concentration, which delightedly fixes on actual phenomena. This means that by eliminating discrimination, distractions, and attachment, one is able to develop quietude, equanimity, and *samādhi*. Second is tranquil concentration manifesting supernatural abilities. This refers to the stabilization that brings forth supernormal powers. Third is tranquil concentration that benefits beings. This is so called because it achieves their benefit, happiness, and *samādhi*. Due to tranquil concentration, one can accomplish skill in mantras to prevent calamities, eradicate epidemics, produce rain, eradicate fear, and bestow food and wealth. One can admonish others to abandon idleness and practice as they should. One has supernatural powers of prophecy, instruction, transformation, illumination, and the elimination of suffering. Thus one is able to eradicate all serious obstructions forever.

The Perfection of Wisdom

Wisdom (*prajñā*) means to discriminate properly in various circumstances. There are three types of wisdom. First is the wisdom that realizes the truth of things as they are. This refers to enlightened awareness of equanimity that realizes the ultimate truth of

selflessness. Second is profound wisdom pertaining to the five fields of knowledge and the three kinds of concentration. By acquiring this knowledge, one is able to quickly attain perfections through a wealth of awareness and realizations. Third is the wisdom of developing compassion and benefiting beings. This means that [the bodhisattva is always] a helpful companion to [sentient beings] and cultivates with them the practices leading to wondrous enlightenment. They study Buddhist doctrines and depend on pure wisdom. 531a
The bodhisattva manifests various forms to benefit the ignorant, guides beings to liberation, praises and encourages the timid, and encourages diligent practice.

Next is the practice of the *four all-embracing virtues:*

1. *Giving.* This has been explained previously.

2. *Kind speech.* This means always speaking pleasantly, mindfully, truthfully, and in accordance with the Dharma. One avoids frowning and maintains a smile. One greets and relates to others graciously, sympathetically instructing them in proper behavior and recognizing qualities of which they are unaware, so that they will realize their own merits. One teaches the Buddha-Dharma in order to benefit them. One generates a pure attitude toward adversaries and vows to dispel the delusions of those who are highly ignorant. One does not reject nor resent those who deceive and wrong the true merit field (i.e., the Sangha, ordained monks and nuns) but employs the difficult practice of speaking kindly to them. Hoping to eradicate their hindrances and obscurations, one teaches the preliminary practices and turns their minds to virtue by expounding the [Four] Noble Truths. One admonishes those who indulge greatly in idleness to abandon their sloth. To those who are skeptical, one explains how to make correct decisions by relying on the four kinds of pure speech and by applying the eight kinds of sacred speech.

3. *Beneficial conduct.* Through kind speech, one first teaches correct principles; then, according to one's understanding [of the Dharma], with a sympathetic and undefiled attitude one encourages, subtly subdues, and establishes others [on the path]. One helps them to obtain immediate benefits and later to obtain wealth

and position; and one further helps them renounce the household life by cutting off desires. One teaches the peace and pliancy derived from abandoning desire. To those who habitually stay near non-virtuous friends, who have not sown the roots of virtue, who have great wealth and position but are extremely extravagant, to those non-Buddhists who cling to wrong views and slander others, and to those who often engage in the eight afflictions and the ten non-virtues, one should teach and help them arouse great compassion. Even when experiencing great hardship, one ignores weariness and generates even greater joy. Even if one has enormous wealth and a high position, one should be as humble as a servant, a slave, an outcaste (*caṇḍāla*), or a devoted child. One is not defiled or hypocritical but is honest and merciful, and this attitude of compassion never degenerates.

4. *Working with others.* Due to the advantages of working with others, if one urges others to study, one must also study oneself. After teaching them the ways of practice, one should practice [these ways] also. Thus the roots of virtue can be established and will not deteriorate. One causes them to reflect: "Whatever is taught is surely beneficial, because the teacher practices it." If not, they are apt to say, "If you yourself are not virtuous, how can you teach me? You still need to receive teachings from others on these things."

Next, one should make *offerings* to the Three Jewels in the following ways:

1. One arranges for offerings to be made to the Buddhas of the present, as well as personally making offerings to relics (*śarīra*s) and *caitya*s (shrines).

2. One makes offerings to the *caitya*s of the other Buddhas of the three periods of time (i.e., past, present, and future) and the ten directions (i.e., in all directions; everywhere), and regards the *caitya*s as the Buddhas although the Buddhas are not of the present.

3. When making offerings to the Buddhas of the present, one reflects:

> "The nature of a *caitya* of a Buddha is equal to that of the *caityas* of all Buddhas of the three periods of time and the ten directions. Therefore, making offerings to a Buddha *caitya* of the present is equal to making offerings to the *caityas* of the Buddhas of the three periods of time and the ten directions."

Thus one makes offerings both to the Buddhas of the present and to those not of the present. If after the Buddha's nirvana one builds one or more Buddha *caityas* as objects of offering, one will
obtain immeasurable great merits, will receive the blessings of the 531b
great Brahma Heaven, will not fall into the evil migrations for countless great *kalpas*, and will fully accumulate merits toward unsurpassed enlightenment.

4. One makes offerings like this in person (i.e., without requesting someone to do it in your place).

5. Out of compassion and in accordance with one's abilities, one gives things to the poor and, hoping for their happiness, encourages them to make offerings.

6. One makes offerings to all [of the above].

7. One offers flowers, incense, and prostrations, as well as valuables and other offerings of wealth, with respect and reverence.

8. One makes many excellent offerings of wealth over a long time and transfers the merit with pure motivation to the achievement of enlightenment.

9. One does not make offerings with arrogance, deceit, negligence, or with impure objects. One makes undefiled offerings of wealth accumulated by oneself or requested from others. One generates [altruistic] aspirations and visualizes transforming oneself into hundreds of thousands of forms to reverently make offerings. Each and every emanation body manifests hundreds of thousands of hands holding fragrant flowers, sends forth hundreds of thousands of songs praising true virtue, and gives hundreds of thousands of wonderful adornments as offerings. One should rejoice in the offerings made in Jambudvīpa as well as in all those made in

the lands of the ten directions. With just a little effort, one can make immeasurably great and extensive offerings. One should generate a virtuous attitude and a joyful mind that diligently pursues this practice.

10. If one properly practices the four immeasurables even for an instant or for a short time with faith and patience, understands the true, inexpressible nature of the Dharma, abides in the nondiscriminating and nonconceptualizing mind, guards and maintains the pure bodhisattva precepts, and furthermore practices the four all-embracing virtues and makes offerings with proper mindfulness, this is a most excellent practice that incomparably surpasses the previous offerings by a hundred thousand myriad times.

When engaged in the practice of making offerings, one should reflect that the Tathāgatas are a great field of merit, have great virtues, and are honored most highly among all sentient beings. They are very rarely encountered, are outstanding in the world, and are the source of reliance. One should regard the Dharma and the Sangha (i.e., with Buddha [Tathāgatas] and Dharma, the Three Jewels) in the same way when making offerings. Thus one can obtain great results which are beyond expression.

Next, one should stay near beneficial friends. A beneficial friend is one who transgresses no precepts; has great learning, practice, and realization; and is compassionate, fearless, patient, tireless, and eloquent. Such are their characteristics. They give benefit and happiness to others, understanding what help is appropriate. They are powerful, employ skillful means, and never tire of benefiting others with impartial selfless compassion. These [actions] are what beneficial friends do. They are scrupulous in their actions, have perfect deportment, are subdued in speech and action, are free of pride and jealousy, are thrifty, and always practice giving whatever they have. Such people are beneficial friends and worthy of trust. Admonishing, reminding [others of virtue], teaching, advising, and expounding the Dharma are the things that beneficial friends engage themselves in for the benefit of beings.

One pays respect and offers service to beneficial friends whether they are sick or in good health. One inquires about their health, greets them respectfully, and lives harmoniously with regard for their activities. One offers them the four daily necessities, frequently requests instruction [from them], and serves them dutifully. This is called "staying near" (beneficial friends).

Next, one should practice the [four] immeasurables. There are three kinds of sentient beings in the Dharma realm. First are those
who neither suffer nor are happy. Second are those who suffer, and 531c
third are those who are happy. Toward these three kinds of sentient beings, one practices [the four immeasurables of] kindness, compassion, joy, and equanimity.

To all sentient beings in the ten directions who wish for happiness, one understands them for what they are and bestows appropriate happiness on them. This is called "kindness dependent on sentient beings." If one practices kindness from the viewpoint of the Dharma, considering sentient beings as conventionally existent, this is called "kindness dependent on the Dharma." If one practices kindness from the viewpoint that all dharmas are not to be discriminated, this is called "unconditioned kindness."

To eradicate the suffering of sentient beings, one practices "compassion dependent on sentient beings." To increase the joy and happiness of beings, one practices "joy dependent on sentient beings." One eliminates the ignorance of those who neither suffer nor are happy, eradicates the hatred of suffering beings, and eliminates the attachments of beings who are happy. Equally one removes all delusions of those [in all three states]. This is called "equanimity dependent on sentient beings." The other [immeasurables] can be expounded similarly.

Among the three immeasurables, the first (kindness dependent on sentient beings) is common in the practice of non-Buddhists; the second (kindness dependent on the Dharma) is practiced by [those of] the two vehicles; and the last one (unconditioned kindness) is only practiced by bodhisattvas. The first three of the four immeasurables (kindness, compassion, and joy) bestow peace and happiness, while the last one (equanimity) brings benefit.

Next, one cultivates a sense of shame and embarrassment. If one does not do what should be done, does what should not be done, covers up one's faults, or performs remorseful actions, one should examine them and develop a sense of shame and guilt with regard to such offenses, respect those who are worthy, and treasure their virtuous actions. This is developing a sense of shame. Observing the traditional modes, feeling ashamed of a bad reputation, rejecting insults, violence, stubbornness, and negative actions, one develops a sense of embarrassment.

Next, one develops perseverance. One brings defiled thoughts under control and is not influenced by delusions. Consequently, although one may undergo great suffering, one practices without a sense of hardship and is undaunted by fears, courageous in the thought of righteousness, and can consistently accord with the true nature of things.

Next, one contemplates the tribulations of the environment, of sentient beings, of afflictions, of views, and of the *kalpa*. One wearies of them and has pity [for those experiencing such tribulations]. Seeing the world in a process of formation and destruction, one develops the thought of impermanence. Realizing that the body is nothing but a combination of the six elements which exists falsely in name, one becomes detached from it.

One greets virtuous elders with respect and treats them as one's own parents. To those whose age and virtues are equal to one's own, one greets and has discussions with them as brothers. One treats inferiors with kindness and encourages them to practice as if they were one's own children. If in a high position, one is never obnoxious with subordinates. One should help those in need according to one's material circumstances. One treats others equally as friends whether they are acquaintances or not, healthy or ill, noble or lowly, rich or poor. One holds no grudges against others but treats them equally as friends. If they make mistakes, one does not chastise them or cause them even a moment's discomfort. One avoids the fourteen defilements by secluding oneself in the six directions, shuns the four kinds of negative companions, and stays near the four kinds of beneficial friends. One shares wealth equally and does not appropriate others' belongings. Appraising the worth of valuables, one does business honestly. Even if others do not realize the value [of an object], one does not even slightly deceive them.

Next, one practices the four reliances. One seeks the meaning [of the Dharma] rather than relying merely on its words; thus fondness and respect for it arise. One relies on the Dharma rather than relying on the person who expounds it; thus the mind abides in its principles. One relies on the sutras in which the meaning is completely revealed rather than on sutras in which the meaning is incompletely revealed; thus one will not be troubled by doubts. One relies on wisdom rather than relying on knowledge; thus one can verify things conclusively. 532a

In short, all the practices, from the four kinds of unhindered understanding all the way to the four profound *dhāraṇīs*, the practices [leading to the accomplishment of the] thirty-two major characteristics, and all the classifications of profound wisdom, are appropriate topics to be studied by a bodhisattva. Through all [three] actions of body, speech, and mind, at all times, one benefits joyfully and unchangingly, without harming or offending. One abides tranquilly in the realization of truth and virtue. With a stable, benevolent mind, one is determined to get free of karmic retribution. One actualizes all the various practices, such as the contemplation on impurity and the thirty-seven practices of enlightenment. Although the bodhisattva practices both vehicles, he does not stop with [the lesser vehicle] (i.e., the Hinayana), as is explained in the sutras.

Next, one should generate the aspiration [for enlightenment for all beings] (*bodhicitta*). This is the original aspiration which encompasses all aspirations, that is, to practice the true Dharma. Again, there are *three aspirations:* (1) to attain understanding of the Dharma in each lifetime; (2) to teach the Dharma to all beings tirelessly; and (3) to sacrifice one's own life and property in order to preserve the true Dharma. Further, there are also *four aspirations:*

(1) to quickly eradicate the suffering of those who have not yet eradicated it; (2) to quickly procure happiness for those who have not yet obtained it; (3) to generate an attitude of eradicating negativity and pursuing virtue in those who have not yet generated such an attitude; and (4) that those who have not yet become Buddhas will soon become Buddhas.

There are also *five aspirations:* (1) generating that exalted mind which initially aspires to attain supreme enlightenment; (2) aspiring to take birth, which means aspiring to take birth in fortunate migrations for the benefit of others; (3) aspiring to practice, which means aspiring with proper motivation and selecting positive actions to be practiced; (4) aspiring properly, which means having the proper aspiration to accumulate all bodhisattvas' merits, both collectively and individually; and (5) *the great aspiration,* including the [following] ten: (a) aspiring to obtain the most excellent objects as offerings to the Buddhas; (b) aspiring to preserve the true Dharma in order to perpetuate it uninterruptedly; (c) aspiring to manifest the eight aspects of a Buddha's life; (d) aspiring to practice all bodhisattva deeds; (e) aspiring to perfectly mature all living beings; (f) aspiring to manifest in all worlds; (g) aspiring to practice to attain all Buddha lands purely; (h) aspiring to see all bodhisattvas incline toward the Mahayana; (i) aspiring that no practice should be in vain; and (j) aspiring to quickly achieve supreme enlightenment. Hoping to actualize the great and extensive results which derive from practice, one should generate these aspirations in each and every action.

The practices and aspirations mentioned above, taken together, constitute the practices of the forty stages. Practicing particular stages, one first generates an attitude of determination to learn the *ten dharmas:* (1) making offerings to the Buddhas; (2) praising bodhisattvas; (3) developing the thought of protecting beings; (4) staying near worthy companions; (5) praising [the virtue of] not retrogressing in the practice; (6) practicing the Buddha's merits; (7) aspiring to be born among Buddhas; (8) training in *samādhi;*

(9) praising renunciation of cyclic existence as a mode of release from suffering; and (10) practicing the ten powers.

Similarly, there are twenty specific practices to be found in each stage; they are expounded in the sutras, but in those stages they mostly involve [continuing to] cultivate previous practices. A few also involve the definitive suppression of afflictions not yet subdued. Before entering the stage of intensified effort, one engages in the practice of the three *samādhis*.

There are two types of dharmas, existent and nonexistent. Both 532b
conditioned and unconditioned dharmas are existent, while self and its possessions are termed nonexistent. Having revulsion for the illusory nature of cyclic existence, conditioned phenomena, and dependent arising, one practices the meditation on desirelessness. Aspiring after the unconditioned, true nirvana, one practices the meditation on non-form. To transcend obsession with attachment to self and the possession of a self and all nonexistent phenomena, one practices the meditation on emptiness. If one speaks only of emptiness, desirelessness, and non-form, it refers to the three branches of learning [in respect to *śīla, samādhi,* and *prajñā*], both defiled and undefiled, both meditative and nonmeditative. If one speaks of the *samādhi* [on emptiness, non-form, and desirelessness], it refers to both the defiled and the undefiled but belongs only to the category of meditative practices. If one speaks of the liberation [resulting from the practices on emptiness, non-form, and desirelessness], it is undefiled and [belongs to the category of] meditative practices. In this stage, these are to be practiced and noted as explained previously.

Next, one practices the four *udānas* (joyful utterances), which were taught in order to purify beings: (1) contemplating that all things are impermanent, being produced and disintegrated; (2) contemplating that all impermanent things are suffering, being compelled [by karma and delusion]; (3) contemplating that the nature of nirvana is peace, being free from the bonds of suffering; and (4) contemplating that all phenomena are selfless in that there is no controller.

Having practiced skillful means, one practices the four contemplations (*vipaśyanās*) in the first two stages—"heat" (*uṣmagata*) and "peak" (*mūrdhana*)—of the path of intensified effort (*prayoga-mārga*); and in the last two stages—"forbearance" (*kṣānti*) and "supreme mundane qualities" (*laukikāgradharma*)—one practices the four true wisdoms. This is the practice of emptiness, which is the practice of benefiting self, leading to the practice of the five immeasurables, which are skillful means benefiting others. In order to benefit others, one first contemplates the sixty-four types of sentient beings and teaches them according to their specific situation. Next, one contemplates the distinct realms in the ten directions and the defilement and purity of the beings that abide in them. Next, one contemplates that there are distinctions of greater and lesser propensities and that some sentient beings possess the ability to be liberated from suffering. Next, one contemplates the fifty-five distinct types of sentient beings to be subdued, and through skillful means one helps them attain liberation.

Next, one contemplates appropriate skillful means. In the "stage of acceleration," one practices benefiting self and others. In the first *bhūmi,* one realizes the truths of the noumenal and phenomenal through undefiled *vipaśyanā;* this is called "insight into the true [of things]," which is realized through meditative practices. It is a meditative practice and has been explained in the abridged form of practice mentioned above.

From this stage onward in the ten *bhūmi*s, one engages in the ten supreme practices, eradicates the ten grave obscurations, and realizes the ten aspects of suchness. The ten supreme practices refer to the six perfections of giving and so forth, plus the perfections of skillful means, vows, powers, and knowledge. All excellent practices are subsumed within these ten. There are twelve types of *skillful means,* of which the first six are internal: (1) caring with compassion; (2) understanding all practices; (3) rejoicing in the Buddha's excellent wisdom; (4) delighting in abiding within cyclic existence; (5) remaining undefiled while transmigrating; and (6) persevering diligently. These next six are external [skillful means]:

(7) causing others to derive immeasurable results through even a little virtue; (8) causing others to amass great roots of virtue with little effort; (9) eliminating anger in those who despise the Holy Teachings; (10) guiding those who remain neutral to become involved; (11) bringing those who are already involved to maturity; and (12) guiding to liberation those who are already matured. These twelve skillful means can be summarized into two: (1) transferring [merit], and (2) liberating [beings].

The five vows can be subsumed under two types: (1) seeking 532c
enlightenment, and (2) benefiting others. The ten powers can be classified into two: (1) discerning and selecting, and (2) training in wisdom. There are two types of pure knowledge which realize all dharmas and establish pure wisdom: (1) enjoying the bliss of the Dharma, and (2) maturing sentient beings.

The practices pursued in the ten *bhūmis* are increasingly superior to those mentioned above. If asked to give up one's body and limbs totally, [a bodhisattva in these *bhūmis*] submits to these wishes with an unstained mind. If someone seeks something which is inappropriate, one would rather give up hundreds of thousands of lives than give something which will be disadvantageous in the long run. If one's motivation is pure and one has a wish to benefit sentient beings, but the being who is asking for one's body and limbs is a vexing demonic force or an insane person, one should not give [up one's body and limbs] to him. When feeling pity for beings who live on discarded food (i.e., hungry ghosts), one should give such food to them. One should not give loved ones (i.e., parents, spouse, children, etc.) away without their consent. Even with their consent, one should not give one's wife and children away to become servants or slaves to those who are cruel and violent. In situations other than the above, one should practice giving.

One would rather commit a most serious offense or transgression, and fall into hell oneself, than cause someone else to perform a negative action. After carefully considering and examining one's good intention, one may even kill a person, but does so with deep regret, shame, and a sense of pity. One casts out tyrannical rulers with skillful means. One prevents theft and returns to their proper owner stolen goods that have been seized by robbers. If [a lay bodhisattva is] not attached or possessive, even impure (i.e., sexual) activities may be allowed if [they] expedite and cause roots of virtue to be sown. Nevertheless, an ordained bodhisattva should not engage in such things.

In order to relieve others of difficulties, one may tell lies or sow discord to keep them away from bad company. One may use abusive language to extricate them from wrong paths or employ vulgar language at an opportune moment to attract them. Through such means, one creates countless merits. One may manifest supernatural powers to frighten those in unfortunate destinies, causing them to abandon transgressions forever. One does not respond to questioning by those with no faith but rather manifests supernatural powers in order to induce faith in them. One intensively benefits them for their complete welfare.

When encountering suffering and oppression, one has no other thought than the realization of patience. One is courageous, tireless, and capable of the ten supreme and inconceivable powers, as well as the meditations appropriate to the various types of beings. At the end of life, one does not reject birth but returns to take birth in the desire realm in order to develop a supreme, impartial, all-pervasive realization of enlightenment. Once one understands the selflessness of all dharmas, one can subdue [sentient beings] expediently and does it in any circumstances without obstruction. In working with others, one may conceal one's own achievements and imposing powers, working together without demonstrating these things. In order to help frightening beings, [a bodhisattva] may even take the transformation body of a dog, even though one is not [a dog]. To those whose roots of virtue are not strong, one actually works together with them in order to strengthen them. However, if one's own practice is lax, one should not use these [last] two methods.

Seeing all Buddhas as equal when making offerings produces an impartial attitude, and with such an attitude one gives the best possible offerings of treasures. If capable of supernatural powers, one manifests immeasurable treasures to others. One gives praise and respect to the Three Jewels in the ten directions in a genuine 533a
way. In practicing the immeasurables, one treats sentient beings equally. One ascertains conventional and ultimate truth, and teaches others to attain this realization. Such immeasurable compassion is called "great compassion" (*mahākaruṇā*). Based on the experience of subtle suffering, one trains in practice for a long time and engages in it boldly. Because the thought of compassion is extremely pure, to cultivate it is to cultivate all the compassionate thoughts of a bodhisattva. Because a compassionate mind is blissful and pure, one with such a mind is very kind to sentient beings, is benevolent toward them, tirelessly endures suffering for them, and is very patient with them. The *śrāvaka*s who have attained their ultimate goal are thoroughly weary of the world, and do not practice this sympathetic attitude as bodhisattvas do. Due to one's practice and the influence of compassion, there is nothing internal or external that [a bodhisattva] is reluctant to give away, and there is no wisdom that cannot be attained. Since the enlightenment of a bodhisattva is based on compassion, one is able to endure all the suffering of cyclic existence. Furthermore, there are the various practices [of the ten perfections] which are related to each of the ten *bhūmi*s, such as the practice of giving in the first *bhūmi* up to the supernatural accomplishments of the tenth *bhūmi,* and so forth. Thus, the ten practices are subsumed under the various stages. That is why ten perfections are enumerated—no more and no less. A verse says:

> Despite hindrances to wealth, nobility, and fortunate
> migrations, and
> Without forsaking sentient beings,
> Increase virtues and diminish faults, and
> Cause others to enter the path of liberation.

Despite hindrances to virtues such as generosity and so forth,
Inexhaustibly and uninterruptedly
Pursue virtue with determination.
Thus, all beings are ripened and good results enjoyed.

The ten hindrances refer to the inherent ignorance which is eliminated successively in the stages of the ten *bhūmis* up through the practice of the ten perfections. Another enumeration of the ten hindrances begins with the hindrance of ordinary appearances of the unenlightened mind and goes up to the lack of complete mastery of all dharmas.

The *ten aspects of suchness* are: (1) universality, which means that one attains equanimity between oneself and others; (2) superiority, meaning that one pursues all practices resulting in renunciation of cyclic existence; (3) supremacy, meaning that one is willing to disregard oneself in the pursuit of the Dharma; (4) nonattachment, meaning that even attachment to the Dharma is eliminated; (5) non-differentiation of types, meaning that one attains the ten pleasant, impartial, pure thoughts; (6) non-defilement and non-purity, meaning one comprehends that [things that result from] dependent arising are neither defiled nor pure; (7) non-differentiation of everything, meaning that one realizes that dharmas are devoid of form and so does not become attached to various phenomena, as is expounded in the sutras; (8) basis of the mastery over phenomena, through which one realizes completely the truth of non-production, not seeing even a single dharma as defiled or pure, as increasing or decreasing; (9) basis of the mastery of all wisdom, meaning that one attains perfect realization and unobscured understanding; and (10) basis of the mastery of all deeds, meaning that one manifests all beneficial deeds as desires.

All bodhisattvas should engage in these practices with *four qualities:* (1) wholesome practice, meaning that one engages in determined, committed, uninterrupted, and faultless practice; (2) skillful means, meaning that one helps others to obtain benefits, practices

proper discipline, accomplishes the tasks received, and teaches the Dharma expediently; (3) benefiting, meaning that one is able to 533b
bestow benefits and happiness when sought; and (4) transferring, meaning that one accumulates roots of virtue derived from [the three] actions [of body, speech, and mind] throughout the three periods of time—and all these accumulated merits, being of one taste and profound, one dedicates with pure faith to the attainment of enlightenment and to no other goal.

One should have *mercy* for sentient beings in seven ways: (1) not causing fear; (2) exhorting them to endeavor in accordance with principles; (3) having a tireless, valiant attitude; (4) [benefiting others] without being asked; (5) not expecting a reward; (6) not giving up even if harmed; and (7) [benefiting others] with boundless impartiality. All of these are referred to as training in the Dharma. Bodhisattvas of the three periods of time should diligently practice these in order to attain unsurpassed enlightenment that is sufficient in itself. Those who have left the household life and their relatives behind and have rejected worldly activities should practice pure conduct, achieve perfect renunciation, and abide by pure morality. Thus, people trust what they say. Laypeople do not have these virtues, so [ordained people] are truly exceptional and deserving of great respect.

Part Two

What has been discussed above are the dharmas to be learned and the ways to practice them. What are the characteristics of those who can learn these dharmas? A bodhisattva's practice comprises twelve abodes that encompass all bodhisattva stages. Only after these stages [have been accomplished] can a bodhisattva attain unsurpassed enlightenment, which is the thirteenth abode of perfect fruition. A verse [enumerating the thirteen abodes] gives them as:

> Inherent nature, the practice of supreme understanding,
> Extreme joy, advanced precepts,
> Advanced mind, three kinds of advanced knowledge,
>   formless effort,
> Formless effortlessness, unobstructed understanding,
> The most perfect bodhisattva abode,
> And the ultimate abode of the Tathāgata.

1. *Abiding in inherent nature.* This refers to the foundation stage before the aspiration for unsurpassed enlightenment (*bodhicitta*) has been aroused. It is only a cause for the other abodes. Its characteristics have been discussed previously.

2. *Abiding in the practice of supreme understanding.* This includes the stages from the initial aspiration up to the first *bhūmi*. From the cultivation carried out in the previous stage, although a bodhisattva has attained purification, he continues to practice for the purpose of further purification. Through differentiating knowledge, he exhorts himself to practice, but he is slow to engage in all practice. Still he encourages himself to preach the Dharma. Although within his own capacities he is able to manifest some degree of correct understanding and to benefit others and make them happy, he has not yet completely learned all practices nor accomplished all fine characteristics, nor purified all thoughts.

3. *Abiding in extreme joy*. This refers to the first *bhūmi*. A bodhisattva in this stage accomplishes all the good dharmas of the
533c previous stages and the ten great vows. It is therefore called abiding in pure and supreme joy. [The bodhisattva] surpasses the state of a common person, realizes the nature of no-birth, is born into the household of the Tathāgata, and becomes a true son of the Buddha. Carrying on the lineage of the Buddha and attaining all kinds of equanimity, he avoids all confrontation and attains true realization and purity. He knows that he is getting closer to enlightenment and has realized the truth of the two kinds of emptiness and the two wondrous wisdoms. Hence, he is overjoyed and practices the ten dharmas so as to abide in purity. The *ten dharmas* are: faith; kindness; compassion; charity; non-indolence; comprehension of all treatises; understanding of the world; cultivation of remorse; perseverance; and making offerings to all Buddhas. [After the completion of these ten practices], he concentrates his efforts to proceed to the cultivation of the other nine abodes.

[In this abode the bodhisattva] often becomes a universal monarch (*cakravartin*) ruling this world [of Jambudvīpa] and subdues stinginess and defilements. He vows, "I resolve to always stay in the most honored position in order to be a refuge for sentient beings and to do beneficial work for them." Or if he takes delight in practicing more vigorously and, further, becomes a monk with pure faith, he can realize hundreds of *samādhi*s in a single moment, see with heavenly eyes hundreds of Tathāgatas in Buddha lands, and comprehend all their transformations. His supernatural power can move hundreds of Buddha lands and his body can emit great light to be universally seen by others. He is able to manifest in hundreds of transformations to benefit hundreds of sentient beings. If he wishes to stay in the world, he can live hundreds of *kalpa*s. He can see things of a hundred *kalpa*s into the past and future, can realize hundreds of Buddhist doctrines, and can transform into hundreds of bodies, each of which manifests hundreds of bodhisattva retinues.

4. *Abiding in advanced precepts*. This is the second *bhūmi*. After achieving the purification of the ten delights in the previous

bhūmi, the bodhisattva enters this *bhūmi.* He is replete with the natural precepts [such as abstaining from killing]. He has little evil karma and does not violate the precepts, let alone commit more or the most serious transgressions. He knows well the causes and effects of actions, and thus exhorts himself and others to practice pure deeds. He has great compassion for suffering sentient beings and comprehends them as they really are. He perceives the Buddha's vast, pure roots of virtue. He often appears as a universal monarch ruling the four continents of the world and stops beings from breaking precepts. His power is ten times greater than in the previous stage.

5. *Abiding in advanced mind.* This is the third *bhūmi.* After penetrating the dharmas practiced in the previous abodes, the bodhisattva enters this abode through ten purifications of the mind through which he penetrates all practices for great enlightenment. He understands that unobstructed wisdom is the only skillful means to eradicate the suffering and afflictions of sentient beings, that there is only nondiscriminating wisdom in the pure Dharma realm (*dharmadhātu*), and that superior *samādhi* is the only way to accomplish this wisdom. He is vigorous in listening to the teachings of the bodhisattva vehicle. He disregards his life and gives up whatever he loves. There are no masters whom he does not vow to serve. He vows to practice all teachings and to endure all suffering. He regards hearing one single verse [about the Dharma] as more precious than treasures filling up the great thousand worlds, and hearing one phrase of the Buddha's teachings, which can bring forth both enlightenment and pure bodhisattva practices, as superior to the attainment of the worldly fruition of a Śakra, Brahma, or universal monarch. If someone were to say to him, "I have a phrase of the Dharma that can bring forth enlightenment and pure bodhisattva practices. If you jump into a firepit, I will tell you [this
phrase]," the bodhisattva would say with willing joy, "I will, even if 534a
the firepit were as big as the three thousand worlds. For the sake of hearing the Dharma, I will jump into it even from the Brahma Heaven, let alone into a small firepit. I would stay in hell a long

time to seek the Buddha-Dharma, let alone undergo just a little suffering." After having this thought, he can practice according to the Dharma and thus abide in the four *dhyāna* heavens of form and so forth. He will then give these up and return [to the world] in order to take rebirth [to help beings] as he wishes. He often becomes a Śakra who teaches beings to cut off desire and covetousness. His power is hundreds of thousands of times greater than before.

6. *Abiding in advanced knowledge corresponding to the modes of enlightenment.* This is the fourth *bhūmi.* After accomplishing the ten dharmas through much hearing, the bodhisattva enters this abode and attains ten advanced wisdoms. He cultivates the dharmas leading to enlightenment that can sever attachment to the view of the self as real and so forth. He abandons slandering and practices praising others. His mind is well regulated and his merits and virtues flourish. Abiding in goodness, he cultivates the practices relating to the basis of discipline and, as a result, perfects wonderful thoughts and superior understanding of the Dharma. The teachings of sages and enemies cannot upset him. He often becomes a king of the Yama Heaven who helps beings eradicate their erroneous views of the self. His power is millions of times greater than in the previous stage.

7. *Abiding in advanced knowledge corresponding to truths.* This is the fifth *bhūmi.* After having achieved the ten joyful and pure thoughts of equanimity, the bodhisattva enters this stage and contemplates all truths with ten skillful means. He correctly refutes all erroneous practices and has compassion for sentient beings. He gathers the provisions [of blessings and wisdom], cultivates proper vows, and practices insightful thought which can increase [virtues] and eradicate deviant thoughts. He employs all kinds of skillful means to bring sentient beings to maturity, such as the arts which can inspire [them to virtue]. He often becomes a divine king in the Tuṣita Heaven who teaches beings to forsake all internal and external deviant dharmas.

8. *Abiding in advanced knowledge corresponding to dependent arising*. This refers to the sixth *bhūmi*. After having realized the nature of equanimity of the ten dharmas in the previous stage, the bodhisattva enters this abode in which he awakens to the teaching of dependent arising which brings about ways to liberation. He cannot be moved by any aberrant thought. In order to benefit sentient beings, he abides in samsara and manifests wisdom and compassion, pursuing unattached wisdom and the perfection of wisdom. He realizes immeasurable superior *samādhis*. His joyful thought cannot be destroyed and nothing can mislead him. He often becomes a divine king in the "Wondrous Transformation" Heaven (*miao hua t'ien*) who eliminates increasing arrogance and so forth, and whose power is hundreds of thousands of millions of times greater than in the previous stage.

9. *Abiding in formless effort*. This refers to the seventh *bhūmi*. After having realized the ten wonderful skillful means of wisdom that lead to superior practice in the world, the bodhisattva enters this abode in which he reaches the stage of the Buddha's uninterrupted and faultless practice. In each single moment, he realizes the ten perfections and other dharmas leading to enlightenment. He engages in and perfects all accelerated practices that are preliminaries to ultimate purity; therefore, this stage is still called defiled [by comparison with the next stage]. The bodhisattva at this stage perfects the skills of the arts and surpasses the meditative states of those of the two vehicles. In each and every thought, he can enter the *samādhi* devoid of the sensation of thoughts and can manifest the most marvelous acts of a bodhisattva. He often becomes a divine king of the Paranirmita Heaven who teaches those of the 534b
two vehicles the skillful means of contemplation. His power is hundreds of thousands of millions of times greater than in the previous stage.

10. *Abiding in formless effortlessness*. This is the eighth *bhūmi*. After having realized the ten foremost wisdoms that penetrate all dharmas, the bodhisattva enters this stage in which he obtains the

pure realization of no-birth through the four true wisdoms (*yathā-bhūta-parijñānam*) cultivated previously. He cuts off the four disasters due to his deep commitment [to eradicate them]. He is awakened and taught by the Buddha's immeasurable ways of incurring wisdom and supernatural powers. He attains the ability to transform into immeasurable bodies; he attains wonderful wisdom and the ten kinds of self-mastery. He obtains superior advantage from what he has been taught. He often becomes a king in the first *dhyāna* heaven. The power of blessings and wisdom from the first moment of entering this abode is double the power accumulated from all previous abodes, and the power from the second moment is two times greater than before. The power increases from moment to moment until he reaches the stage of the tenth *bhūmi*. It is difficult to describe [this power] exhaustively.

11. *Abiding in unobstructed understanding*. This refers to the ninth *bhūmi*. Because the bodhisattva is not satisfied with the previous abode, he penetrates further and takes delight in the supreme nature of wisdom. He arouses wisdom, accelerates his practice, and discourses upon the Dharma. He preaches the Dharma and practices according to the truth. He thus becomes a great Dharma master with unobstructed understanding. He often becomes a king in the second *dhyāna* heaven.

12. *Abiding in the foremost perfection of the bodhisattva*. This refers to the tenth *bhūmi*. After attaining the purity of unobstructed understanding in the previous abode, the bodhisattva is fit to become a Dharma king and to receive consecration in the Dharma. He is able to attain immeasurable kinds of concentration without defilement. He does what the Buddha does, and obtains wonderful bodies and retinues equal to those of a Buddha. He attains great brightness, realizes the wisdom that works for the benefit of sentient beings, and acquires immeasurable *dhāraṇīs* for liberation, supernatural powers, insight, and other innumerable merits such as these. He often becomes a king of the gods (Maheśvara) of the formless realm. Equipped with provisions for the bodhisattva

path, he is able to accept the great, subtle Dharma rain from the great Dharma cloud of the Buddha. His enlightenment, which is like a great cloud, can shower down the rain of the Dharma that washes away dust and helps roots of virtue grow and ripen.

The extermination [of afflictions], the practices, the realizations, and the merits of each abode are not exclusive. They vary in each abode according to different degrees of perfection. The bodhisattva abode in the practice of supreme understanding tends to follow the practice of formlessness. This practice is still narrow, imperfect, and indefinite, while in the next six abodes [the bodhisattva] achieves the practice of formlessness and his practice becomes broad, faultless, and definite. In the last four abodes, the bodhisattva perfects the realization of purity and attains the fruition of his measureless practices. At the sixth abode in the practice of supreme understanding and faith, he does not backslide in faith and his roots of virtue cannot be destroyed. In the seventh abode, the bodhisattva's mind does not retrogress and he never reverts to either of the two vehicles. In the abode of ultimate joy, he never retreats from nor forgets his realizations. In the abode of formless effortlessness, he can progress in his practice with no 534c
effort. Whatever he does, he does only to seek wisdom and to bestow benefit and happiness. Therefore, the bodhisattva knowingly keeps some delusions and thus willingly takes rebirth. This is why he does not exterminate all afflictions. There are five kinds of births:

1. *The birth that eradicates calamities* (*saṃśamanī-utpatti*). This means that through the mastery of vows, the bodhisattva takes birth as a great fish in order to feed the hungry, as a great doctor to help the sick, as a peacemaker to skillfully settle conflicts, as a great king to properly eliminate suffering, or as a great god to sever deviant views and acts. [He can transform into] fire, water, conveyances, boats, and so forth in order to avert disaster for various beings.

2. *Birth of the same kind* (*sabhāga-anuvartinī*). Through the power of self-mastery derived from vows, the bodhisattva may take

birth [even] in the unfortunate realms of the animals and so on. However, he does not do evil as other beings do but does good that they do not do. For example, he goes to a tavern to help the drunken and to a brothel to show the faults of lust. He discourses upon the true Dharma to help rid beings of faults.

3. *Noble birth* (*mahāsattva-utpatti*). This means that a bodhisattva is naturally born with supreme qualities, such as long life, pleasant appearance, nobility, and riches, with which he severs sentient beings' arrogance and other faults.

4. *Advanced birth* (*ādhipatya-utpatti*). This means that the bodhisattva takes birth as one of the ten kings in order to teach sentient beings as needed.

5. *Final birth* (*varamā-utpatti*). In this birth a bodhisattva perfects his provisions [for enlightenment]. For example, Maitreya will take birth in the household of a brahman national master, and Śākyamuni took birth in a *kṣatriya* household. [In his final birth] the bodhisattva manifests the attainment of Buddhahood and accomplishes all Buddha deeds.

The bodhisattva also encompasses sentient beings with four acts:

1. *Sudden and universal gatherings.* This means that at the time of arousing the initial aspiration for enlightenment, the bodhisattva universally encompasses all sentient beings as his retinue and resolves to do his best to benefit them.

2. *Increased gathering.* If the bodhisattva is the host of a family, he encourages his parents [to do good], he is aware of their kindness and favor, and he is filial to them. He provides his wife and children with necessities and he does not oppress his servants but is patient with them. When they are sick, he consoles them and cares for them as he would for himself. He does not belittle them. If he is a king, he does not punish people with weapons but benefits them with the Dharma and with valuables. He depends on his own lands for livelihood and does not invade other lands. He sees sentient beings as his own parents or children. He speaks truthfully, does not cheat, exhorts others to forsake evil, and teaches them to practice virtue.

3. *Inclusive gathering.* This means that the bodhisattva equally and impartially takes in beings, but not for the purpose of fame, benefit, or service. He draws in his followers with undefiled thoughts. It is for their benefit that he teaches them proper practices. He does not trick them with false practice.

4. *Gathering at proper times.* This means to draw in and bring to maturity all sentient beings of inferior, medium, and superior faculties at the appropriate time, either for a long or short period of time.

The thirteen abodes are included in the seven *bhūmi*s: (1) the *bhūmi*s of inherent nature (*gotra*), (2) of supreme understanding and practice, and (3) of pure supreme bliss—these three *bhūmi*s correspond to the first three abodes; (4) the *bhūmi*s of cultivating proper practices, which correspond to the next six abodes; (5) the definite *bhūmi* (*niyata-bhūmi*), which corresponds to the tenth 535a
abode, for it falls in the third definite *bhūmi;* (6) the *bhūmi* of definite practice, which corresponds to the eleventh abode; and (7) the ultimate *bhūmi,* which corresponds to the twelfth and thirteenth abodes because both cause and fruit are perfected.

Although the practices of a bodhisattva discussed previously are immeasurable, they can be classified into four kinds: (1) the practice of perfection, such as the six perfections or ten perfections (*pāramitā*s); (2) the practices leading to enlightenment (*bodhyaṅga*), such as the thirty-seven factors of enlightenment, the four reflections, and all other wonderful practices; (3) the practices of supernatural powers, such as the six kinds of supernatural powers; and (4) the practices that bring sentient beings to maturity. Beings to be subdued are immeasurable and so are the skillful means [to fulfill this task].

The practices explained above concerning the object of practice, the method of practice, and the practitioners are all [encompassed by] bodhisattva practices. To courageously and earnestly cultivate and yet not to perceive the form of cultivation is what is meant by practice (*hsing*).

Why are the practices said to be "profound"? The Madhyamikans comment that because the subtle doctrine [of *prajñā*] is profound and inconceivable, those of the two vehicles cannot comprehend it and common people cannot fathom it. Therefore, it is said to be profound.

The Yogācārins comment that ultimate truth (*paramārtha-satya*), whether in its [function of] cognition (*chih; jñāna*) or as an object of cognition (*ching; viṣaya*) is beyond words and speculation. It cannot be referred to by analogy and is so subtle that it is difficult to comprehend. It is replete with three unsurpassed qualities and seven characteristics. In its functioning it greatly benefits all beings, like a vast ocean of virtuous dharmas or a pool of wondrous treasures. No one except the great enlightened Lord of the Dharma Realm (i.e., the Buddha) can be said to have realized [ultimate truth]. Therefore, the practices to be cultivated are said to be profound, and the bodhisattva should diligently seek to realize them.

[Another interpretation is that] it is difficult for the bodhisattva to perfectly realize the true form of suchness, to obtain illuminating wisdom, to express teachings in words, to achieve myriad practices, and to penetrate the existence and emptiness of the field of objects of cognition (*viṣaya-gocara*). The perfection of wisdom is foremost and the others are supplementary. They are called "*prajñā*" and are therefore profound.

What is meant by "*when*" [in the second line of the *Prajñā-pāramitā-hṛdaya-sūtra*]? The Madhyamikans comment that conventionally a bodhisattva arouses faith and cultivates in order to penetrate the truth of emptiness, while ultimately he realizes that the nature of dharmas is emptiness and cultivates wisdom (*prajñā*). The time at which the practice is perfected is what is [indicated in the text] by "when."

The Yogācārins comment that unsurpassed enlightenment is broad and profound and cannot be attained with little effort. With regard to the [thirteen] abodes expounded previously, if counted in nights and days, it would take innumerable hundreds of thousands of millions of great *kalpa*s or even longer to realize each and every abode. Or, if counted in great *kalpa*s, which are beyond

all measure, then it would take three immeasurable great *kalpa*s to accomplish perfect realization. During the first immeasurable great *kalpa,* each practice is cultivated separately until the abode of ultimate joy is realized. During the second immeasurable great *kalpa,* within each practice all practices are cultivated until the abode of formless effortlessness is realized. With the purification of mental disposition and the definite vigor during the third immeasurable great *kalpa,* all practices are cultivated in all stages 535b
until the abode of the Tathāgata is realized.

For those who are constantly vigorous, it may not necessarily take so long. If the bodhisattva is extremely vigorous, as if standing on tiptoe, he can perhaps skip many medium or great *kalpa*s but definitely not the immeasurable great *kalpa*s. Therefore, in the causal stages, the bodhisattva has to go through various practices completely for three immeasurable great *kalpa*s before the attainment of enlightenment, for it is only then that the five perfections are achieved. This is to say that the cultivation of the five aspects of wisdom is divided into stages of three *kalpa*s or is divided into stages according to the individual's mentality. When the practice [of *prajñā*] is perfected, this is [what is indicated in the text] by *when.* When the bodhisattva gets insight into emptiness, he will properly realize wisdom. Since he practices through stages, he has to go through them all. The *pratyekabuddha,* who has sharp faculties, still has to go through hundreds of *kalpa*s of practice, let alone anyone who seeks Buddhahood but has not yet been equipped through many *kalpa*s of preparation.

SUTRA: [KUAN-TZU-TSAI] HAD AN ILLUMINATING VISION OF THE EMPTINESS OF ALL FIVE SKANDHAS, AND SO FORTH.

Commentary: This passage shows that from the practice of profound wisdom the bodhisattva has obtained the eye of wisdom. *Illuminating* (*chao*) means penetrating into emptiness. The conditioned dharmas, such as form, feelings, and so on, are within the confines of the three periods of time and are either external or internal, gross or subtle, inferior or superior, close or distant.

Skandhas (*wen*) mean the aggregates, which include form, feeling, perception, impulses, and consciousness. *And so forth* (*teng*) refers to other dharmas such as the sense fields (*āyatana*).

The Madhyamikans comment that the previous [passage of the sutra is to] break attachment to the perceiving subject by revealing its emptiness, while this passage is to break attachment to the perceived object by revealing its emptiness. If one is obstructed by ignorance and confused about the principle of *paramārtha,* and falsely takes the *skandhas* and others as existent, one is like a person who believes images seen in a dream to be real. If one correctly comprehends the principle of ultimate truth (*paramārtha-satya*) and does not become attached, one is like a person who awakes from a dream and realizes that the phenomena [seen in the dream] do not exist. Therefore, the practice of *prajñā* can illuminate the empty nature [of phenomena].

The Yogācārins comment that although all practices are nothing but the practice of *prajñā,* realizing the true and expelling the false come from the wisdom that illuminates emptiness. Therefore, the text emphasizes this point. The word "emptiness" here signifies the three non–self-natures: the substance of everything with the nature of mere imagination (*parikalpita*) is nonexistent and lacks self-nature; therefore, it is said to be empty. [The nature of] "arising dependent on others" (*paratantra*) [is analogous to the following:] form is like foam, feeling is like floating bubbles, perception is like the shimmer of heat (e.g., as in a desert mirage), impulses are like the plantain (i.e., hollow on the inside), consciousness is like the tricks of a conjurer; since they are unlike the way they are grasped [in ordinary perception] and lack a self-creating nature, they are also called "empty." According to another interpretation, it is the absence of *parikalpita* in *paratantra* that is the true nature (*pariniṣpanna*), which is why the latter is called "empty." Actually, the three natures are neither empty nor non-empty. The implicit intent of calling them empty is to break attachment. The reason the last two (i.e., *paratantra* and *pariniṣpanna*) are called empty is not because they are completely nonexistent. Buddha's implicit intent in calling them all empty is to indicate, in general, that [both] existence and nonexistence are said to be empty. The Buddha said:

> The ultimate truth is that the production of form
> is devoid of self-nature.
> I have already taught that.
> Anyone who does not know the esoteric intention
> of the Buddha
> Loses the right path and cannot proceed to enlightenment.

Furthermore, this emptiness is the essence of suchness, the 535c
nature of which is neither empty nor existent but is revealed through emptiness. In order to counteract attachment to existence, emptiness is spoken of provisionally (*prajñapti*). Foolish people who do not understand this assert that the five *skandhas* and other dharmas are definitely devoid of true existence; hence they discriminate between them (i.e., true existence and the *skandhas*). To trace them back to their original substance, they are nothing but suchness. For apart from the noumenal, the phenomenal has no separate nature. Therefore, a sutra claims that all sentient beings possess the *tathāgatagarbha,* and all dharmas are nothing but suchness. The [sutra] claims that phenomena having marks (*lakṣaṇas*) are empty, without marks, in order to make sentient beings cut off the bond of marks.

There are *five kinds of eyes:* (1) the eye of flesh, which [sees], without meditation, the constructed pure forms; (2) the divine eye, which sees pure forms constructed by meditation; (3) the eye of wisdom, which is the wisdom that illuminates the principle of emptiness; (4) the Dharma eye, which is the wisdom penetrating the teachings; and (5) when the previous four [eyes] are fully awakened, they get the name "Buddha." In the causal stages, [the bodhisattva with] the wisdom eye penetrates emptiness and contemplates clearly. This is called "illuminated vision." However, in the stage of preparation, to get insight into the nature of emptiness, he hears and reflects on it. This is mainly a practice of faith and understanding. Only after the stages of intensified cultivation does he exclusively cultivate contemplation. Although in both stages the bodhisattva's insight into emptiness is called "illuminating," he has not yet realized the truth, because it is still accompanied by [attachment to] marks. In the tenth *bhūmi,* when he arouses the contemplation without defilement that penetrates truth, this is truly "illuminating emptiness." In the stage of the Tathāgata, illuminating is perfected and he knows that the object of cognition (*viṣaya*) beyond words is provisionally (*prajñapti*) called "empty." Although emptiness includes both the emptiness of self and dharmas, in order to teach Śāriputra only the emptiness of dharmas is mentioned here, because Śāriputra's attachment to the self has long been eliminated and need not be eradicated. Or, since attachment to the self arises due to attachment to dharmas, if one contemplates the emptiness of dharmas, the self will become empty, too.

Although the substance of emptiness has no distinctions, it appears differently in phenomena. According to the *Mahāprajñāpāramitā-sūtra,* there are sixteen kinds of *emptiness:* (1) the emptiness of internal elements; (2) the emptiness of external objects; (3) the emptiness of both internal elements and external objects; (4) the emptiness of the great; (5) the emptiness of emptiness; (6) the emptiness of ultimate reality; (7) the emptiness of the conditioned; (8) the emptiness of the unconditioned; (9) the emptiness of the ultimate; (10) the emptiness of the unlimited; (11) the emptiness of non-dissipation; (12) the emptiness of original nature, (13) the emptiness of all marks; (14) the emptiness of all dharmas; (15) the emptiness of non–[self-]nature (*wu-hsing k'ung; niḥ-svabhāva-śūnyatā*); and (16) the emptiness of the self-nature of non–[self-]nature (*wu-hsing-tzu-hsing k'ung; niḥsvabhāva-svabhāva-śūnyatā*). Or, it is said that there are seventeen kinds of emptiness, that is, [the sixteen emptinesses above] plus the emptiness of nonattainment. Or, there are eighteen kinds of emptiness, including the emptiness of self-nature (*svabhāva-śūnyatā*). Or, there are nineteen kinds of emptiness, including both the emptiness of the highest object-support (*ālambana*) and the emptiness of mutual nonexistence. Or, there are twenty kinds of emptiness; that is, of the eighteen emptinesses, the emptiness of non-dissipation is divided into the emptiness of dissipation and the emptiness of the unchangeable, and the emptiness of marks is expanded to the emptiness of own-mark (*svalakṣaṇa*) and the emptiness of general mark (*sāmānya-lakṣaṇa*). A verse explains:

The eater and the eaten,
These depend on a body and where it abides.
Anyone seeing the principle like this
Has found the two truths of emptiness.

For the sake of benefiting sentient beings,
So as not to reject samsara,
And in order to perform good [deeds] without limit,
Thus one contemplates these as emptiness.

For the purification of inherent nature, 536a
For the attainment of good marks,
And for the purification of the Buddha-Dharma,
The bodhisattva contemplates emptiness.

Pudgala (person) and dharmas
The real nature of both does not exist.
This is the nature of their non–[self-]nature.
Therefore, the two emptinesses [of self and dharmas]
  are specifically established.

SUTRA: THUS, HE OVERCOMES ALL SUFFERING AND ILLS.

Commentary: The Madhyamikans comment that this passage briefly explains that when the two attachments [to self and to dharmas] are severed and the two emptinesses are revealed, all suffering can be overcome. Attaining insight into the emptiness of [self-]nature and getting away from discrimination are like a moth coming out of a cocoon, leaving behind its bondage forever. One can then overcome all suffering and ills and quickly realize nirvana. Although ultimately there is nothing to be overcome or attained, conventionally there is something to be overcome and attained.

The Yogācārins comment that through insight into the emptiness of [self-]nature, one can transcend cyclic existence (samsara). [This passage] reveals the benefit from previous practices and the "third fortification of mind"; [the bodhisattva] contemplates overturning the basis (*āśraya-parāvṛtti*), which is deep, subtle, and difficult to realize. If he is thinking of withdrawing [from practice], he should fortify himself thus:

> "Sentient beings in the world who practice crude forms of giving and other practices can incur superior fruition at the end of life, let alone I who now cultivate unobstructed and wondrous virtues. Would I not realize the overturning of the basis that overcomes suffering, just like others who, through the practice of wisdom, overcome suffering, forsake coarse afflictions, and attain freedom from afflictions? So, I should do the same."

He thus encourages himself to increase practice. He does not belittle himself or retrogress.

Overcomes (tu) means to transcend. *Suffering* means that sentient beings and the worlds of the three realms are produced from the afflictions of karma (*karma-kleśa*s), are contaminated (*sāsrava*), and are nothing but suffering. There are generally three kinds of suffering. All contaminated dharmas are by nature transient, oppressive, and disturbing. These are called "suffering [resulting] from karmic conditioning" (*hsing; saṃskāra*s). All worldly pleasures will eventually come to an end. Whatever dependently arises [through conditions] is bound by suffering. [Pleasure and pain] are both called "suffering caused by destruction." The suffering whose nature is oppressive and which causes unbearable and repeated pain is called the "suffering of suffering." This suffering refers to all disasters and adversities.

There are also eight kinds of suffering. The suffering from abiding in the womb, coming out from the womb—these are the roots of suffering and are called "suffering caused by birth." The decay caused in the course of time is called "suffering from old age." That the body becomes weak and sick is called "suffering from sickness." That life comes to an end is called "suffering from death." The appearance of the undesired is called "suffering from encountering what one hates." When a loved one has departed, this is called "suffering from parting from what one loves." Not getting what one wants is called "suffering from unattained desires." All contaminated *saṃskāras* are called "everything gathered into the five *skandhas* of appropriation" (*pañca-upādānaskandhāḥ*).

Ills (*erh*) refer to the eight difficulties, fears, the three minor calamities, and so forth. Due to failure to attain insight into emptiness, one clings to the marks of objects of cognition (*ching hsiang*), develops discrimination in the mind, and produces afflicted actions. [As a result,] one suffers birth in the five destinies. Once a person sees the three types of non-natures as empty or perceives that the *skandhas*, [*āyatanas*, *dhātus*,] and so on are the emptiness of suchness and does not develop discrimination, that person can eradicate evil effects and consequently transcend and overcome all suffering and adversities. A verse says:

> The bonds of the marks binding sentient beings, 536b
> Who are bound by the crude barriers (*dauṣṭhulya*)
> Only by cultivating both calm (*śamatha*) and insight
> (*vipaśyanā*) well
> Can they be totally liberated.

Depending on the true, one gains insight into emptiness through which illusory karma is overcome. Through overcoming suffering, fruition manifests in great magnitude. The mark of emptiness is illuminated through hearing and reflecting on the teachings in the stage of preparation. In the sixth stage of the tenfold mind, faith does not backslide and the wholesome roots (*kuśala-mūla*) cannot be severed. Hence, the most serious suffering and ills are subdued forever. Therefore, a verse in a sutra says:

> If there is anyone in this world who accomplishes
> The highest correct view,

> Although he might have to go through thousands of transmigrations,
> He will not fall into the evil destinies of rebirth.

After the fourth of the ten abodes, the crude barriers and ignorance do not occur and the suffering and ills of the evil destinies can be subdued. In the "abode of acquiring the Tathāgata nature," the bodhisattva eradicates afflictions without remainder forever, leaves behind birth and death, and transcends the three realms. The *Sutra on Pratītyasamutpāda* (*Yüan-ch'i-ching*) says:

> The *saṃskāra*s of non-Buddhists and ordinary people are conditioned by four kinds of folly. If Buddhists and ordinary people are lazy [in applying themselves to overcoming the barriers], their "fortunate" (*fu*) and "not moving" (*pu-t'ung*) *saṃskāra*s are conditioned by three types of folly. Those who are not lazy, I would not say they are conditioned by ignorance. Therefore, after this stage all suffering and ills of the evil destinies are subdued.

After the seventh abode, the bodhisattva does not retrogress and leaves behind all the suffering and ills of the two vehicles. In the stage of penetrating understanding, he first realizes true emptiness and then overcomes all suffering, the ills of the three evil destinies, and the eight kinds of affliction. Or [some sutras say that in this stage] the bodhisattva can forever leave behind all the suffering, ills, fears, and afflictions of the three realms. [Some others claim that] it is only in the eighth *bhūmi* that he is rid of the ills, for until the seventh *bhūmi* some afflictions remain. In the tenth *bhūmi* insight into emptiness is perfected, all defiled seeds are eliminated forever, and the suffering [resulting from] from mortal changes are all exhausted. In the stage of the Tathāgata, he benefits sentient beings. The bodhisattva manifests to benefit beings from time to time, while actually he has not [yet reached the stage of the Tathāgata].

Kuan-tzu-tsai Bodhisattva has not yet become a Buddha; however, because of his insight into emptiness, he will certainly eradicate [all suffering]. *Overcomes all* is said to encourage the arousal of aspiration.

SUTRA: ŚĀRIPUTRA,

Commentary: The Madhyamikans comment that beings are established through dharmas, and dharmas are the cause of beings. Here the emptiness of beings is revealed first and then that of dharmas.

The Yogācārins comment that in the following portion of the text, Śāriputra is mentioned as one who responds [to the teachings] and as an example, to show the superior practice of eradicating the four barriers. The following section of the text can be divided into three parts. The first part, beginning with "*Śāriputra,*" is to present the teachings on emptiness generally. The next part, beginning with "*therefore,*" is to show specifically what should be seen as empty. The last part, beginning with "*because of non-attainment,*" is to expound the principle of emptiness.

The Sanskrit word *śāri* refers to a kind of small, freshwater bird. Śāriputra is so named because of the eloquence of his mother [Śarikā]. Also, to show that he was the son [of Śarikā], he was called *putra* (son). Because his mother was quite skilled at debate, her son was named after her so as to defend good and destroy evil. Śāriputra 536c
understood much even from hearing only a little. When the Buddha expounded teachings [on emptiness], Śāriputra was the first to comprehend [them]. Now, when the sutra expounds the doctrine of emptiness, he is called upon as an example. Only the supreme teaching that encompasses all dharmas is expounded to show the principle of emptiness. Although only the venerable [Śāriputra] is called upon as one who is responding [to the teachings], actually a multitude is included, too. They are called upon but they have not awakened to emptiness. Therefore, they are first encouraged and then urged to eradicate the four barriers [of desire, anger, fear, and ignorance].

SUTRA: FORM DOES NOT DIFFER FROM EMPTINESS, AND EMPTINESS DOES NOT DIFFER FROM FORM. FORM ITSELF IS EMPTINESS, AND EMPTINESS ITSELF IS FORM.

Commentary: The four elements and their productions, such as the ten "spheres of form" (*rūpa-āyatana;* i.e., the five sense organs of the eye, ear, nose, tongue, and body and their associated sense objects of shape, sound, smell, taste, and touch) and the "sphere of dharma" (*dharmāyatanikāni rūpāni;* i.e., the five types of conceptualized forms), whose nature is to constantly change in the present, are generally called "form."

The Madhyamikans comment that this passage extensively expounds the emptiness of dharmas. The *Mahāprajñāpāramitā-sūtra* states:

> Why is that? Form is by nature empty, for it does not need to be emptied. The emptiness of form is not form, yet form is not apart from emptiness, and emptiness is not different from form. Form itself is emptiness, and emptiness itself is form.

This is to break two kinds of attachment. The phrase "form does not differ from emptiness, and emptiness does not differ from form" is to break attachment to the notion that apart from conventionally grasped form (*grāhya-rūpa*) there is true emptiness. Beings do not understand true emptiness and thus cling to form, erroneously increase deluded karma, and revolve in samsara. Now, [this passage] shows that the form of a flower seen through a cataract is actually caused by the diseased eye and is nothing but empty existence. Ultimately, form does not differ from emptiness. According to the Holy Teaching, whatever dependently arises is completely empty.

"Form itself is emptiness, and emptiness itself is form." This is to break foolish people's views that it is only when form has become nonexistent that it becomes empty. People permit various discriminations with regard to form and emptiness. Now, according to the ultimate teaching, form is originally empty by nature. [But] there is a distinction between how the emptiness and form of objects (*artha*) and mental images (*bimba*) are understood at the deluded and awakened stages.

Why does one have to wait for the destruction of form to see emptiness? It is like an [imaginary] flower seen [with an eye that has] a cataract; the flower is by nature nonexistent. Why should one have to wait for the destruction of the flower for it to become empty? Therefore, one should not be attached to form or emptiness; rather, one should eliminate erroneous views so that nirvana can ultimately be attained. What these two sentences of the sutra mean is that form is by nature empty; it is not that form becomes empty only after it is destroyed.

The Yogācārins comment that, according to ultimate truth, all dharmas are empty and nonexistent. Although this sounds reasonable at first glance, actually it is not necessarily so. The true and the conventional mutually shape each other, for if the conventional is not existent, the ultimate ceases. Form and emptiness are mutually dependent, for if form ceases, emptiness disappears. Therefore, the substance of form is not originally empty.

The Madhyamikans comment that actually emptiness is neither empty nor not empty. It is for the purpose of turning confusion into understanding that form is said to be empty. It is not that the emptiness of form is definitely empty, for emptiness is also empty.

The Yogācārins comment that if form produced through conditions is originally nonexistent, then the fool would originally be wise, and common people and a sage would be mutually interchangable. If we all consider ourselves teachers, who are the confused?

The Madhyamikans comment that afflictions (*kleśa*s) become enlightenment. Samsara is nirvana. The troubles of the world are 537a
the seeds of Tathāgatahood. All sentient beings are originally in quiescence. Are not the foolish originally wise?

The Yogācārins comment that [there are two extremes: one claiming that form and emptiness are radically different, and the other claiming that they are identical.] If one asserts that things of form (*se-shih; rūpa-vastu*) are separate from the principle of emptiness, then one [can] reject form as delusion and seek emptiness [alone] for enlightenment. If [on the other hand] emptiness already is originally form, wisdom becomes identical to stupidity (*yü*). [If so,] wouldn't it be perverse to seek wisdom and reject stupidity? Furthermore, why abhor samsara and seek nirvana if pain (*duḥkha*) and pleasure (*sukha*) are not distinct? [If they are the same,] what is the use of seeking nirvana? Stupid people (*yü fu*) in samsara would have already attained nirvana, and sages seeking the highest accomplishment would be committing heretical error.

The Madhyamikans comment that worldly affairs, delusion (*mi*) and awakening, seeking the state of a sage, and forsaking worldliness are all ultimately empty, so why [should one] seek one and forsake the other?

The Yogācārins comment that if the phenomenal is allowed to be called nothing but emptiness, then in ultimate truth there is self-contradiction, because it would be as if the unenlightened realize that form is emptiness, while the enlightened do not realize the emptiness of form; that the diligent sages are pitiable and detestable, and the indolent and foolish are admirable. The Buddha said, "How does a bodhisattva comply with the perfection of skillful means?" If sentient beings do not understand the sutra in which the Buddha expounds all dharmas as devoid of self-nature, existent things, production and extinction, and as like an illusion and a dream, then the bodhisattva should explain to them that the sutra does not mean all dharmas are nonexistent; rather, it means that only the self-nature of dharmas is nonexistent. Therefore, all dharmas are said to be devoid of self-nature. Although there are designations of things depending on [whatever level of] discussion is yet possible, according to ultimate truth, their expressible nature is not their own true nature. Therefore, it is said that all dharmas are nonexistent.

If in theory the self-nature of all dharmas is originally nonexistent, what then is produced and what is destroyed? Hence, all dharmas are said to be neither produced nor destroyed. Illusions and dreams are not real or existent as they appear, but it is not that their shapes or images are nonexistent. Similarly, all dharmas are not as real and existent as foolish people habitually think they are, and yet it is not that all dharmas, though ultimately beyond language, are, in themselves, entirely nonexistent. When one awakens to the fact that all dharmas are neither existing nor nonexisting, this is like [awakening] from an illusion or a dream whose nature is nondual (i.e., dream realities are neither entirely existent nor nonexistent). Therefore, it is said all dharmas are like an illusory dream.

With regard to all dharmas in the Dharma realm (*dharmadhātu*), the bodhisattva does not become attached to or forsake them even a little bit, nor does he increase, decrease, or destroy them. If the dharmas are truly existent, he sees them as existent, and if they are truly nonexistent, he sees them as truly nonexistent. To instruct others like this is what is meant by the bodhisattva's complying with skillful means.

What the above passage means is that foolish people get at- 537b
tached to either the notion that the self-nature of dharmas substantially exists, or to the notion that [all dharmas are] without self-nature, like an illusion and a dream, without existence or production and extinction. It is not that sagely knowledge does not exist. The Dharma-nature beyond words of the objects of cognition (*viṣayas*) of the ultimate and conventional truths is not like an illusion or a dream, whose shapes and images and essence are totally nonexistent, and called non-nature, and so on. Understanding that "what is attached to" (*parikalpita*) is nonexistent is called awakening to what is not existent; and understanding that the objects of cognition [cognized by the] sage (*ārya*) exist is called awakening to what is not nonexistent. Therefore, the sutra says that the bodhisattva does not become attached to what is nonexistent, nor does he forsake what is existent even a little bit. He understands what is nonexistent as nonexistent, and what is existent as existent. If one [erroneously] understands according to the ultimate truth that the substance of dharmas is empty and not existent at all, this is not skillful means. If one claims that enlightenment is not nonexistent and thus does not forsake it even a bit, this is also a vain supposition, for it diminishes and loses the actual truth.

Therefore, this passage of the sutra is aimed at breaking attachment to the existence of form, as previously [explained], and thus it says that form is empty. Emptiness means nonexistence (*wu*). It is not that Dharma-nature is empty; rather, what the foolish attach to as inherent nature when sensing the marks of form does not exist. The attachment to [the notion of the] nonemptiness [of form] and [the attachment to the notion that] form becomes empty only after it is destroyed are two erroneous views. They should be eliminated. [This passage of the sutra] reveals the true meaning of form in distinction from what people [conventionally] understand. One should not develop erroneous sentience and perverted views. When erroneous sentience is cut off, grasped forms disappear. Therefore, one should break attachments to whatever arises from dependent nature (*paratantra*) and mere imagination (*parikalpita*). This is just as when the cataract is removed, the [imaginary] sky-flower [seen through a diseased eye] disappears. The activities (*tso-yung*) of the reality which the two vehicles and non-Buddhists cling to as Dharma-nature produced by causes and conditions are not existent at all. Therefore, the Holy Teaching claims that the causally produced dharmas are empty, but this does not mean that illusory forms of dependent nature are all empty. A verse says:

> The nature of erroneous discrimination (*parikalpita*),
> Can be established because of this [interpretation].
> It is neither substantially existent nor totally nonexistent,
> So that the cessation [of defilement] and liberation are
> possible.

The Holy Teaching again claims that all dharmas are not produced by themselves nor by others, nor by both themselves and others, nor not by both themselves and others. Although there are no causes and effects to grasp on to, there are attainable functions and effects. Otherwise, there will be no conventional truth; and if there is no conventional truth, there is no ultimate truth either. Depending on whom, then, can one attain liberation? Or, this emptiness refers to the emptiness of the Dharma-nature. If one holds the notion that the form attached to by mere imagination and the form of dependent nature are definitely different from true existence, then one sees that the true and the conventional definitely discriminate against each other. This can easily cause confusion. [The text] now reveals that the nature of the two forms is empty, without marks, unconditioned, and does not account for cognition (*chih; jñāna*) or objects of cognition (*viṣaya*s). One should get rid of the two attachments and seek true emptiness. Therefore, resorting to emptiness, one can eliminate both erroneous views. The form of Dharma-nature, in itself, is the true mark (*chen hsiang*), which is not different from emptiness and is nothing but emptiness. What doubt can there be?

The two truths of the Holy Teaching are different in depth. They mutually contain the true and conventional aspects, including: "worldly conventional convention," "worldly conventional truth," "truly true truth," and "truly true convention." The con- 537c
ventional is the convention of the true, and the true is the truth of the conventional. Where there is the conventional, there is the true. When the conventional is not existent, neither is the true. It is not that there is emptiness apart from form, and it is not that form and emptiness are definitely the same or different from each other. Therefore, true emptiness and form are neither different nor not different and neither the same nor not the same. To counteract [the view that they are] definitely different, [the sutra] says that they are the same and not different. However, [the sutra's assertion that they are] the same and not different also means that they are not the same nor not different. The *Madhyāntavibhāga*[-*śāstra*] says:

> The unreality of both [object and subject],
> And the reality of this unreality are
> Neither existent nor nonexistent,
> Neither different nor the same.
> This is characteristic of emptiness.

Now, [the sutra] speaks of the mutual revelation of form and emptiness in order to make the meaning clearer and to break doubts and attachments. Previously, the name of Kuan-tzu-tsai was mentioned in order to fortify the mind; now form and emptiness are spoken of in order to eradicate the *four barriers:*

1. The thoughts of [those of] the two vehicles are narrow and inferior, for they loathe the world and do not take delight in benefiting others.

2. They erroneously infer and arouse doubts with regard to the Mahayana.

3. When hearing, reflecting, [and meditating] on the term "self," they give rise to a plethora of dharma attachments.

4. They become attached to the discriminations in the provisional explanations of the teachings presented to them, from the lowliest pieces of form all the way up to *bodhi*.

Now, the sutra's proclamation that form and other aggregates are not different from emptiness is to make one eradicate the inferior thoughts of [those of] the two vehicles and other hindrances so that one can obtain nondiscriminating wisdom and achieve the transcendent practices.

SUTRA: SO ARE FEELING, PERCEPTION, IMPULSES, CONSCIOUSNESS, AND SO FORTH.

Commentary: Fearing that people might hold the wrong notion that only form is not different from emptiness, and only the substance of form, not the others, is empty, the sutra further mentions that feeling and so forth are empty, like form. *Feeling* refers to the unpleasant, pleasant, or neutral sensations that are experienced through contact with the physical world. *Perception* means to conceptualize the distinctions between marks and no-marks, small and large, immeasurability and scarcity. *Impulses* refers to good, bad, and neutral volitional thoughts and all other mental activities. The mind, thought, and perception are capable of making distinctions and they are generally called "consciousness," which includes the four abodes of consciousness and the consciousness able to abide in them. From form comes feeling, from feeling comes perception, from perception comes action, and from action comes comprehension.

Therefore, the sequence is from form to feeling and so forth.

Because people grasp the five aspects with regard to the self—self-body, self-feeling, self-speech, self-activity, and self-substance—[the sutra says that] the *skandhas* have only function but no self-nature, for the self and its possessions are nonexistent. [The sutra] only says that the five [*skandhas*] are neither decreasing nor increasing. Foolish people do not understand that in order to break attachment to the self (*ātma-grāha*), the sutra provisionally speaks of *skandhas* while actually there are no existing *skandhas*. Thus, they hold them as existent. To counteract this wrong notion, [the five *skandhas*] are said to be empty. The *Viṃśatikā* (*Twenty Verses*) says, "Sentient beings have no self but only causes of the dharmas."

And so forth refers to the five kinds of skillful means with regard to the [twelve] sense fields and the [eighteen] realms. The *Mahāprajñāpāramitā-sūtra* says, "From form up to enlightenment, everything is empty. Even if there is a dharma that surpasses nirvana, I will say it is still as an illusion or a transformation." 538a
Therefore, the phrase "and so forth" (*teng*) encompasses all dharmas. The Madhyamikans and Yogācārins have the same interpretation in regard to this.

The *Mahāprajñāpāramitā-sūtra* says, "The self-nature of feeling, perception, impulses, and consciousness is empty and does not need to be emptied." It then goes on to expound extensively that feeling, perception, impulses, and consciousness are empty, and emptiness is feeling, perception, impulses, and consciousness. Why is this so? *Bodhi* is nothing but a designation and is therefore called "emptiness." So are form, feeling, perception, impulses, and consciousness.

SUTRA: THEREFORE, ŚĀRIPUTRA, ALL DHARMAS ARE MARKED WITH EMPTINESS: THEY ARE NOT PRODUCED NOR EXTINGUISHED, NOT DEFILED NOR IMMACULATE, NOT INCREASED NOR DECREASED.

Commentary: The previous passage indicates the emptiness of the substance of dharmas, while this passage indicates the emptiness of the referent (*yi; artha*) of dharmas. *All dharmas* refer to those of form, feeling, and so forth. *Produced* means to come into being from what is originally not existing. *Extinguished* means that which temporally existed before no longer exists. *Defiled* refers to the taint of hindrance; its opposite is called *immaculate.* When form is broadened, it is *increased;* its opposite is *decreased.*

The Madhyamikans assert that according to conventional truth, since form and other dharmas are existent, they are produced and so forth. According to the ultimate truth, form and so forth are originally empty. How can they be produced from emptiness? Therefore, the empty forms of production, extinction, and so forth are nonexistent.

The Yogācārins say that whatever dharmas are produced from mere imagination (*parikalpita*) and dependent nature (*paratantra*) are devoid of self-nature. The essential nature of form and so forth is empty in substance. It does not have the characteristics of production and so forth to which those of the two vehicles are attached. Therefore, [the sutra] says that the emptiness of form is neither produced nor destroyed and so forth.

Furthermore, if one clings to the notion that the mutability of the conditioned is definitely produced and destroyed, that the unconditioned before and after its transcendence of bondage substantially possesses [the qualities] of defilement and purity respectfully, and that before and after enlightenment the conditioned and the unconditioned decrease and increase respectively, then one is holding on to strong attachments. Therefore, substance and form are all nonexistent. How could it be like the attachments of [mundane] people [who see] that the conditioned is produced and extinguished, and that the unconditioned is defiled and purified? The principle is the same with "increase" and "decrease." This is like seeing a mirage [and believing it to be] real water. The mistaken water is originally empty; how can it be produced? Nonetheless, [the image of] water appears [in the distance due to] the sun's blaze.

Again, someone might rebut: If the phenomena of dependent nature are by nature empty, and if they are produced and extinguished, this [emptiness] should also be [produced and extinguished]. The answer to this is that, just as forms arise and cease in the sky (*t'ai-k'ung*) but the marks of emptiness are absent, similarly although *paratantra* has arising and ceasing, true emptiness is not like that.

Again, someone might rebut: If all dharmas are nothing but true emptiness, the mark of emptiness pervades defilement such as greed and pervades purity such as faith; then it should be either defiled or pure. The answer to this is that just as in space, form is either pure or defiled, but not so with the mark of emptiness, so although dharmas are pure or defiled, the mark of emptiness is not so. A verse says:

It is neither defiled nor undefiled,
Neither pure nor impure.
The nature of mind is originally pure
But is tainted by adventitious defilement.

Perhaps someone might rebut: If dharmas are all true without 538b
distinct marks, and if the sweet, dewlike Holy Teachings increase and decrease, then so should true emptiness. The answer to this is that, just as in space, the marks of form increase and decrease but not the marks of emptiness, so the Holy Teachings increase and decrease, but not the nature of emptiness. This is due to the difference between noumena and phenomena and between substance and marks. If all dharmas are nothing but emptiness and suchness, how can there be phenomena such as increasing, decreasing, and so on?

What is expounded above generally indicates that not only is the substance of form not different from emptiness, but the differentiations produced from form are not different from emptiness. Here only three sets of dualities (i.e., produced and extinguished, defiled and immaculate, increased and decreased) are negated, while actually they are not exclusive with regard to the form of emptiness.

The *Mahāprajñāpāramitā-sūtra* says that self-nature is neither produced nor extinguished, defiled nor pure. When a bodhisattva practices *prajñāpāramitā,* he does not see arising or ceasing and he does not see defilement or purity. Why? It is because designations are expediently used to distinguish various dharmas. However, following the establishment of designations, discrimination and attachment arise accordingly. When the bodhisattva practices *prajñāpāramitā,* he does not perceive all [designations]. Because he does not perceive them, he does not give rise to attachment.

SUTRA: THEREFORE, IN EMPTINESS THERE IS NO FORM, FEELING, PERCEPTION, IMPULSES, NOR CONSCIOUSNESS.

Commentary: The Madhyamikans comment that the previous passage expounds the undifferentiation and identification of form with emptiness. For fear of an unclear meaning, and in order to make [one become] skillful in contemplation, the text indicates other dharmas which also do not exist in emptiness. *Therefore* is used to continue the passage and to indicate that in emptiness there are no other dharmas.

The Yogācārins comment that those of the three vehicles generally practice five kinds of skillful means, namely, the [five] *skandha*s, the [twelve] sense fields (*āyatana*s), the [eighteen] realms, dependent arising, and the [Four Noble] Truths. According to their own need, they practice either "close contemplation" or "distant contemplation." Since those of the two vehicles are attached to existence, nonexistence is expounded to counteract it. The substance and the referent (*artha*) of what one attaches to as emptiness are both made tranquil; therefore, the nature of what is attached to as *skandha*s is nonexistent. Nevertheless, the Buddha expediently set up the conditioned dharmas as *skandha*s and broke [the attachment] to the five aspects regarding the self so as to lead [people] to gradually enter true teachings. This is just skillful means; it does not mean [that the dharmas are] truly existent. Hence, a verse says:

> [The conditioned dharmas are] like the starry cataract,
> Illusion, dew, bubbles, dreams, lightning, and clouds
> Which come into being from the combination of conditions.
> One should perceive them like this.

Even the conditioned dharmas are not determined *skandhas*; how much less can attachment to *skandhas* be true? The nature of the Dharma is empty; therefore, it is without the mark of the *skandhas*. Hence, there are no five *skandhas* in emptiness. The *Mahāprajñāpāramitā-sūtra* says:

> Furthermore, Śāriputra, when bodhisattvas practice the *prajñāpāramitā,* they should contemplate like this: "Bodhisattva" is nothing but a designation; *"prajñāpāramitā"* is nothing but a designation, so are form, feeling, perception, impulses, and consciousness.

The sutra goes on to expound extensively. 538c

SUTRA: NO EYE, EAR, NOSE, TONGUE, BODY, MIND; NO FORM, SOUND, SMELL, TASTE, TOUCHABLES, NOR OBJECT OF MIND,

Commentary: This passage indicates that there are no twelve sense fields (*āyatanas*) in emptiness. The Madhyamikans comment that the Buddha expediently spoke of the [twelve] sense fields to lead [beings] to the true. After having led them to the true, he spoke of emptiness according to its true meaning.

The Yogācārins comment that it is only through contact between the sense organs and sense objects that the six consciousnesses arise. This is what is meant by sense fields. The worldly phenomena include seeing [through the eye], greeting [through the ear], smelling incense [through the nose], tasting food [through the tongue], serving [through the body], and discerning [through the mind]. The Buddha spoke of the sequence of sense fields like this:

In the causal stage, the eye and ear do not reach what they are able to grasp (i.e., they do not directly contact their objects but perceive them from a distance). Nose, tongue, and body do reach what they are able to apprehend (i.e., they have direct contact with their objects). Intentional thought (*manas*) is the eight consciousnesses. In the effect stage, both sets [of senses] are karmically indeterminate (*pu-ting; aniyata*). The function of the eyes and ears is superior, and so gets the name "divine." Their transformations are unreal, only [active in] the desire and form realms. The consciousnesses of the lower realms depend on the higher realms through which karma, conditions (*pratyaya*), supernatural power, concentration, and the power of the Dharma arise. According to different stages of attainment, their functions are accordingly inferior or superior. [The arising of the eye consciousness requires] nine conditions; [the ear consciousness,] eight conditions; [the consciousnesses of nose, tongue, and body,] seven conditions; and [the mind consciousness,] five conditions.

Form refers to manifestation, shape, and appearance. *Sound* refers to the noise produced either through contact with the "great elements" [earth, water, fire, and wind] or without contact with the "great elements." *Smell* refers to natural, combined, and changed odors. *Tastes* refers to the bitter, sour, sweet, hot, salty, and mild [flavors]. *Touchables* refers to the four elements and that which is created by the four elements. *Mental dharmas* refers to the dharmas that do not "resist" each other (*apratigha*), other mental activities, elements not associated with the mind, and the unconditioned. The first five [organs] have only the two characteristics [of ripening (*vipāka*) and nourishing (*aupacayika*)]; and the rest (i.e., the mind) also have the characteristic of outflows (*niṣyanda*) [in addition to the two characteristics mentioned above]. *Vipāka* exists only in the realms of desire and form, while the other two exist in all three realms. Form and sound are manifested, and mind and its objects have all three [characteristics]. The ten kinds of form are either karmically indeterminate (*avyakta*) or beneficial (*kuśala*), and are provisionally designated (*prajñapti*) according to either their separation from or dependence on existence. All [sense fields] are either defiled or nondefiled. The *Viṃśatikā* says:

> Conforming to the beings of birth by transformation,
> Out of hidden intention, the World-honored One
> Said there are sense fields of form and so forth,
> Which are just like beings of transformational birth.

This [verse] means that for [those] beings who falsely cling to the existence of self and thus have long been immersed in the cycle of samsara, but who do not wish to seek liberation and take the improper as a guiding principle, the Buddha, in order to counteract their nihilistic views, taught with secret intention that there are beings of transformational birth so as to lead them to enter the true and abandon clinging to a self. Those of the two vehicles who do not understand [the Buddha's] expedient teaching hold it as true. Now the text shows that which is clung to is originally nonexistent. Since there are no true sense fields in the dharmas of dependent arising, their external forms are also nonexistent, because the nature of dharmas is empty. To continue from the previous passage, this passage concludes that the sense fields are nonexistent. The *Mahāprajñāpāramitā-sūtra* says, "The sense of the eye is nothing but a designation, so are other senses up to that of dharmas. The sense of the eye is empty; so are the other senses up to that of the objects of mind."

SUTRA: NO SIGHT-ORGAN REALM, AND SO FORTH, UNTIL WE COME TO NO MIND-CONSCIOUSNESS REALM.

Commentary: This passage indicates that in emptiness, there 539a
are no eighteen realms (*dhātus*). The Madhyamikans comment that the elements of eye, form, and eye consciousness; ear, sound, and ear consciousness; nose, smell, and nose consciousness; tongue, taste, and tongue consciousness; body, touchables, and body consciousness; and mind, dharmas, and mind consciousness are [collectively] called "the eighteen realms."

Here [the passage mentions only] the first and last realms to cover all [eighteen]. Conventionally, they are said to be existent; ultimately, they are nonexistent and are only designations, because their self-nature is empty.

The Yogācārins comment that because the sense organs and the sense objects can support the six consciousnesses and have the relation of cause and effect among themselves, they are called "realms." The realms of consciousness arise according to the sequence of the sense fields. Therefore, the eighteen realms are in this particular order. The six sense organs that come in contact with their objects are called "the six internal realms." The objects of the sense organs—eyes and so forth—are the six "external realms," and the senses that result from contact between the organs and their objects are the six consciousnesses. Among them, the realm of mind consciousness refers to the mind (*hsin*), mental consciousnesses (*yi*), and consciousnesses (*shih*). Mind denotes the eighth consciousness (*ālaya-vijñāna*), which holds the "seeds" (*bījas*) perfumed [by karma] that take rebirth. Its nature is good and non-covered (*wu-fu; anivṛta*) and it can transform the body receptacle, which is considered the base of sentient beings. It has three meanings: (1) considered as attached to the self, it is called *ālaya,* which means "store," for it can store, is stored, and is the object of attachment; (2) considered as the effect of good or bad karma, it is called *vipāka* (*hsi-shou*), for it is the result of good or bad deeds; (3) considered as continuously holding together [karma], it is called *ādāna,* meaning holding together, in that it maintains the sentient organism.

Denoting the seventh consciousness that holds on to the defiled characteristics of self, *mentation* (*manas*) is the basis of contamination (*āsrava*); it is pure and always equalized, and good (*kuśala*) but covered (*nivṛta*). It also has three names: (1) considered as responding to attachment to the self, it is called "covered *manas,*" for it takes the *ālaya* as the self; (2) considered as responding to attachments to dharmas, it is called "non-covered *manas*" since it holds dharmas when they are in the condition of *vipāka* (i.e., ripening, or reaching maturity; *vipāka* is always karmically neutral); (3) considered as having the nature of cogitation and intellectualization, it is simply called *manas,* because through *ādāna* (attachment) it gives rise to thinking and calculating. The cognizer (*ālambaka*) and the object-support (*ālambana*) are equal. Both the seventh and eighth consciousnesses have three names: Their first two [names] are contaminated (*sāsrava*), while their third name has the characteristics of noncontamination (*anāsrava*).

Consciousness (*vijñāna*) denotes the first six consciousnesses. Their names are self-explanatory [in their meaning]. They all have the three [good, bad, and undefiled] characteristics. In the stage of Buddhahood, the *ālaya* is transformed into great mirror wisdom (*mahā-ādarśa-jñāna*), because it manifests the [illusory] images explained through nine similes.

In the first *bhūmi, manas* is transformed into the wisdom of equality (*samatā-jñāna*), which possesses the characteristics of ten equalities. In the stage of insight of those of the three vehicles, the sixth consciousness is transformed into the wisdom of profound contemplation (*pratyavekṣaṇā-jñāna*), which is perfected with ten superior functions. The first five consciousnesses are transformed into the wisdom of perfect achievement (*kṛtyānuṣṭhāna-jñāna*), which brings forth the fulfillment of the ten actions and the original vows.

In the causal stages, one characteristic of the consciousnesses is discrimination, while in the resultant stage [discrimination is] eliminated, so they are called "wisdom." The eight consciousnesses encompass the seven mental realms. The fourth wisdom, (i.e., great mirror wisdom) is solely wholesome and classified as belonging to the Dharma realm. The third wisdom illuminates existence and emptiness and encompasses ultimate and conventional knowledge. 539b
The wisdom of performed action illuminates conventional, not true, knowledge. Great mirror wisdom and the wisdom of equality are forever immovable. The former is perpetual and pervasive and is also called "omniscient" (*sarvajña*). The wisdom of profound contemplation and the wisdom of perfect achievement are sometimes interrupted. Although these four wisdoms possess various qualities (*guṇa*s), according to their own characteristics their qualities increase differently.

The Buddha spoke the Dharma in both brief and extensive ways. With regard to the meaning of *skandha*s, form and consciousness were briefly explained, while the [meaning of] the sense fields and the [eighteen] realms was extensively explained. When mental activities are broadly explained, the meaning of sense fields and realms is briefly explained. For the sake of unintelligent people of the three vehicles, the *skandhas* are said to be conditioned, the sense fields are said to include two attachments [i.e., attachment to the internal six sense fields and the external six sense fields], and realms are said to include the objects of attachments [in addition to the twelve sense fields]. In order to break attachment to self, they are provisionally called "realms" (*dhātus*). Those of the two vehicles do not understand [the Buddha's intention], and thus cling to the realms as real. Actually, what they are clinging to is empty. Continuing from the previous passage, these [eighteen realms] are also negated.

SUTRA: NO IGNORANCE, NO EXTINCTION OF IGNORANCE, AND SO FORTH, UP TO THERE BEING NO OLD AGE AND DEATH, NOR NO EXTINCTION OF OLD AGE AND DEATH.

Commentary: The Madhyamikans comment that the previous passage indicates no "distant contemplation," and the next passage no "close contemplation," while this passage indicates that there is no "close contemplation" for the *pratyekabuddha*. Therefore, a sutra says that for anyone seeking the solitary enlightenment [of the *pratyekabuddha,*] the twelve links of dependent arising are taught. There is another interpretation. From ignorance up to old age and death, these are only designations because their self-nature is empty. Therefore, they are said to be nonexistent. *Extinction* means emptiness. Emptiness is also empty. Hence, the sutra says, "No extinction of ignorance and so forth, up to there being no old age and death, nor no extinction of old age and death." The twelve links of dependent arising are neither existent nor empty. The same is true of the others, which can now be reflected [from the example of the first link].

The Yogācārins comment that Maitreya said there is a forward (*anuloma*) and a reverse (*pratiloma*) way to view these [links of dependent arising] from both defiled and pure aspects. The forward way is to perceive defilement in accordance with the cycles of birth and death, while the reverse way is in accordance with increasing practice [to break the links]. The forward way of perceiving purity is based on the severance of the fundamental hindrances, while the reverse way is based on repeated contemplation after severance.

The forward way of perceiving defilement is, first, to perceive that the substantial nature [of life] contains *twelve links* (*nidānas*): (1) *ignorance* (*avidyā*), meaning to be deluded about the internal and foolish (*yü*) about the external; (2) *karmic conditioning* (*saṃskāra*), which means [moving on to] fortunate or unfortunate [circumstances or rebirths] or not moving [up or down in the next life]; (3) *consciousness* (*vijñāna*) means the karmic-maturing (*vipāka*) consciousness; (4) *name and form* (*nāmarūpa*), meaning the five *skandhas*; (5) *six sense spheres* (*ṣaḍāyatana*), meaning the six sense organs; (6) *sensory contact* (*sparśa*), meaning contact with objects; (7) *feelings* (*vedanā*), meaning painful and pleasurable sense objects; (8) *desire* (*tṛṣṇā*), referring to clinging to the three realms; (9) *appropriation* (*upādāna*), meaning afflictions (*kleśas*); (10) becoming (*bhava*), meaning the seeds—[developed] from "karmic conditioning" up to "feeling"— moistened by desire and appropriation, [engendering fruit that] leads from one existence to another; (11) *birth* (*jāti*), the reappearance of suffering resulting [from previous existence]; and (12) *old age and death* (*jarā-maraṇa*), that is, [the physical] changing, weakening, and ending of life.

Next, one should contemplate that erroneous actions produced from ignorance can result in the consciousness that manifests [seeds of] past karma. Then, the characteristics of the five *skandhas* appear and the sense organs develop. After contacting and feeling the field of objects of cognition (*viṣaya-gocara*), the "seeds" establish results. Indulging in desires, one increases *kleśas* that in turn "moisten" previous karma. [Consequently] the suffering of the five destinies (*gati*)—birth, old age, death, sorrow, and misery—arise. Therefore, the sutra says ignorance conditions *saṃskāras* and so forth, until we come to birth conditioning old age and death. The five links of consciousness and so forth are not necessarily in sequence and, therefore, according to whatever 539c should arise, they become the condition for the arising of their next link. The reverse way of perceiving defilement is to contemplate in accordance with the established [Four] Noble Truths. That is to contemplate the suffering of old age and death, the cause of old age and death, the cessation of old age and death, and the practice resulting in the cessation of old age and death. In the same fashion (going backward to birth, then becoming, and so on), the other links should be contemplated.

Because the link of old age and death comes under the truth of suffering, among the [twelve] links of dependent arising one contemplates it in reverse at first. With three kinds of characteristics, one looks into the link of old age and death: (1) "subtle dependent arising"; (2) "coarse dependent arising"; and (3) "not undetermined." The causal conditions that bring about birth are called "subtle dependent arising," namely, craving, grasping, and existence. Birth itself is called "coarse dependent arising," that is, the link of birth. Due to these two kinds of dependent arising, old age and death are brought forth.

"Subtle dependent arising" is the cause of old age and death in future lives, and "coarse dependent arising" is the cause of old age and death in the present life. Except for these two kinds of dependent arisings, there is nothing that can bring about the result of old age and birth. This is called "not undetermined."

Although one might contemplate the truth of suffering of old age and death, this does not cover [contemplation on] the truth of the cause resulting in future suffering brought about by craving. Therefore, one should again look into the factors and conditions of the cause of present suffering, that is, contemplate in reverse the links of feeling, contact, the six "places" (i.e., sense organs), name and form, and consciousness. To contemplate future suffering is [contemplation of] the truth of suffering, and to contemplate the cause of [the factors and conditions that bring about suffering] is [contemplation of] the truth of the cause [of suffering].

When looking into the cause through which the cause of future suffering originates, one realizes it is due to past causes that present suffering arises. After understanding that [present suffering comes from] past causes, one would no longer wonder how [present suffering] comes into being. Because consciousness and name and form are like bundles of reeds, which depend on each other without one being dominant, one contemplates the links of consciousness after that. Thus, contemplation of [the truth of] suffering and its cause, whether forward or backward, covers only ten links.

Next, one should contemplate the truth of the cessation [of suffering] from old age and death up to ignorance. How can all [suffering] completely cease? It is through not creating new karma caused by ignorance that suffering can cease.

Next, one should seek the ways leading to the cessation [of suffering]. One should try to remember the teaching on dependent arising as taught by the Teacher (i.e., the Buddha) so that the proper view with regard to the world and wisdom can manifest. To contemplate again and again in this way causes the proper view to increase. These are the forward and reverse ways of perceiving defilement.

Employing the previously accumulated provisions of proper view, one gradually attains the pure and wise views of the *śaikṣa*s (i.e., those in training for enlightenment, but not yet enlightened) and arhats. One can thus completely cut off ignorance, craving, and also birth caused by ignorance. Within the present situation, one can realize wisdom and liberation. Because feelings, [dharmas] associated with mind (*citta-samprayukta*), craving, and afflictions are severed, one realizes liberation of the mind (*cetovimukti*). When ignorance ceases, [the links of] karmic conditioning (*saṃskāra*s) and consciousness down to feelings do not arise. Therefore, a sutra says that because ignorance ceases, karmic conditioning ceases, and so on up until we come to [the link of] sensory contact ceasing; then feeling ceases. Since feeling does not arise, there is nothing to cause desire. Hence, it is said that when feeling ceases, desire ceases, and all sorrows and miseries likewise cease. What is left is nothing 540a
but purified consciousness that abides in the realm of "nirvana with remainder." This is called the realization of nirvana in the present. When all contaminations are eliminated one abides in the traces of

the eternal truth, which is called "nirvana without remainder."

The reverse way of perceiving purity is to look backward into the way of destroying [endless samsara]; that is, what should be destroyed so that birth and death cease to arise? [From this contemplation] one realizes that if dependent arising is inoperative, the seeds (*bījas*) [of past actions] and present activities are both nonexistent, so old age and death, [which would otherwise result from past and present actions,] are also nonexistent. When the impermanent conditions that give rise to [the seeds of the past becoming present activities] cease, then old age and death cease. Likewise, if dependent arising is inoperative, then the proclivities (*anuśaya*), delusions, and ignorance do not exist, and thus karmic conditioning does not exist. When ignorance that is conditioned by impermanence ceases, karmic conditioning ceases. These are the reverse and forward ways of perceiving purity. [Some interpretations of] the forward way of perceiving defilement do not include the link of birth, because it awaits the opportune moment [to arise]. The reverse contemplation only covers nine [links], because [the link] of consciousness is not taken as a cumulative condition. Or, [one may] contemplate eleven links, since [the link of] ignorance is without cause and lacks the seed of wisdom.

The Buddha expediently set up [the teaching on the twelve links of dependent arising] so that the *pratyekabuddha*s can attain *bodhi* by themselves. But they do not understand and mistakenly hold on to the reality of the dependent arising of defilement and purity. Now, [in this sutra, the twelve links] are said to be nonexistent, so that attachment to them can be forsaken. Of the defiled aspect it is said, "There is no ignorance, up to there being no old age and death." Of the pure aspect it is said, "There is no extinction of ignorance, up to there being no extinction of old age and death." The reverse way of observation should be done in the same fashion as the forward way. Once the existence of the first link is negated, so are the other links [one by one in sequence].

Although a bodhisattva in the sixth *bhūmi* observes in this fashion, he still holds on to the reality of the production and extinction [of the twelve links]. Only after the seventh *bhūmi* is a bodhisattva rid of the notion of production and extinction. *Production* denotes defilement observed from the forward way of contemplation; that is, to observe "no ignorance up to no old age and death." *Destruction* denotes purity observed from the reverse way of contemplation, that is, to observe "no extinction of ignorance up to no extinction of old age and death." What is negated here is the attachment to the two types of dependent arising as eternally abiding (existent). [The sutra] does not negate that dependent arising operates (*kung-neng*) in principle. This is why a sutra teaches that through conventional truth, one enters ultimate truth, and that although there is no reality of the doer [of karma], karma [nonetheless] exists.

It is not that the nature of dependent on others (*paratantra*) is the definitive (*ting*) mark of dependent arising, while the destruction of ignorance, and so on, is the true principle. Therefore, [the sutra] negates both [extremes]. If good and evil karma are entirely nonexistent, the sutra should only say that dharmas are not existent. Why then does it also explain in detail that they are not nonexistent? Depending on causes and conditions, dharmas are established. This teaching itself is very important, and thus it should be explained in detail.

SUTRA: NO SUFFERING, NO CAUSE, NO CESSATION, AND NO PATH.

Commentary: The Madhyamikans comment that the previous passage denies the "close contemplation" of the *pratyekabuddha,* while this passage denies the "close contemplation" of the *śrāvaka.* Therefore, a sutra says that for those who seek [the fruition of] a *śrāvaka,* the Four Noble Truths are expounded. It further says that the Four Noble Truths are merely a designation, since they are empty of self-nature. However, these two passages address the same object. [Practicing contemplation] on dependent arising includes 540b
the practice of contemplating the Noble Truths. Therefore, once [the existence of the twelve links of] dependent arising is negated, the [Four Noble] Truths would be as well.

The Yogācārins comment that the *Śrīmālādevī-sūtra* speaks of the four "established Noble Truths" and the four "unestablished Truths." These eight Noble Truths are unknown to those of the two vehicles. Birth and death resulting from karma in the three realms is called *suffering*. Affliction and defiled actions are the *causes* [of suffering]. Nirvana is the *cessation* [of suffering], and ways bringing forth the realization of the wisdom of emptiness is the *path*.

The established Truth denotes what is known through coarse, obvious, and shallow knowledge. Birth and death resulting from change is *suffering*. The obstacle of the known (*jñeyāvaraṇa*) and undefiled discriminative karma are the *causes* [of suffering]. Non-abiding nirvana with pure nature is the *cessation* [of suffering,] and the ways to the realization of the wisdom of the empty nature of the dharmas is the *path*. The non-established Truth is subtle, hidden, and difficult to comprehend.

Combining these two explanations (established and nonestablished Noble Truths), generally speaking, oppression by contamination is *suffering*. What causes future existence is called the cause [of suffering]. Hence, the neutral dharmas [which are neither good nor bad] do not belong to the truth of the cause [of suffering]. This is a brief explanation of birth and death as effects of causes. The four kinds of nirvana denote the *cessation* [of suffering]. The uncontaminated conditions (*anāsrava-saṃskṛta*s) of the way to realize the cessation [of suffering] is called the *path*. This is a brief way of explaining transcendence of the world as the effect of causes. Just as a patient should know his own illness, the cause of his illness, the cure, and the methods (dharmas) of the cure, so [should a person] contemplate the suffering of samsara, the cause of suffering, the cessation of suffering, and the methods [leading to the] cessation [of suffering]. Only what sages cognize can truly be called the "Noble Truths."

There is another interpretation. One can contemplate nothing but the suchness of the two emptinesses. This is a contemplation based on the synthetic view. Each of the Four Noble Truths has its own four practices, namely, impermanence, suffering, emptiness, and selflessness; causes, accumulation, production, and condition; cessation, calmness, subtlety, and detachment; and path, suchness, practice (*hsing*), and transcendence.

From the practices of the truth of suffering, the four perverted views (*viparyāsa*) can be eradicated. In order to get insight into truth, one has to contemplate through intensive practices not only suffering but also the "unestablished truth" from which one gets insight into the truth. The Buddha spoke of suffering and so forth, while actually there is no suffering and so forth. The *śrāvaka*s do not understand this, so in order to break their attachment [the sutra] says that there is no suffering and so on. Since dharmas of dependent nature are not necessarily a mark of suffering or the cause of suffering, how can they truly be differentiated? Therefore, [the Four Noble Truths are] negated. Although [a bodhisattva] in the fifth *bhūmi* contemplates like this, he still holds the coarse forms of defilements and purity as real. It is in the sixth *bhūmi* that he removes the obstacles derived from attachment to defilement and purity. Defilement is contamination. Without attachment to it, one realizes the two truths of suffering and the causes of suffering. Purity is noncontamination. Without attachment to it, one realizes the two truths of cessation and the path.

SUTRA: THERE IS NO KNOWLEDGE AND NO ATTAINMENT.

Commentary: The Madhyamikans comment that the previous passage negates the "close contemplation" of the *śrāvaka,* while this passage negates the "close contemplation" of the bodhisattva. The way that leads to realization is called "knowledge," and the object [of practice] realized is called "attainment." Where there is realizable knowledge, there is attainment. Realizable knowledge is empty; so is attainment. A sutra says that for those who seek bodhisattva-hood, the six *pāramitā*s are taught. However, the sutra also speaks of no knowledge and no attainment. If dharmas are not empty, then when at first there is practice, later there will be attainment. Since dharmas are nonexistent, then when there is no

540c practice in the first place, later there will be no attainment. The *Mahāprajñāpāramitā-sūtra* says that all kinds of knowledge are empty and even the unsurpassed *bodhi* is also empty.

The Yogācārins comment that the bodhisattva contemplates only the nonestablished [truths], hence, generally speaking, [in terms of] the "close" [contemplation], there is no "knowledge" nor "attainment." A verse says:

> Since the existence of consciousness is apprehended
> (*suo-te; upalabdhi*),
> Nonexistence of sense objects is apprehended.
> Since the nonexistence of sense objects is apprehended,
> The nonexistence of consciousness is apprehended.

When one realizes suchness through nondiscriminative cognition (*nirvikalpa-jñāna*), the mind and objects of cognition (*viṣaya*) are unified and equal. The grasper (*grāhaka*) and the grasped (*grāhya*) are nonexistent. In subsequent wisdom (*pṛṣṭhalabha-jñāna*), there is no bondage from forms, illusory grasping, nor the two kinds of attachment. Another verse says:

> Due to the nature of apprehending the existence of
> consciousness
> And establishing that nothing is apprehended,
> Hence know that in apprehending existence of the two
> (i.e., consciousness and its object),
> They are equally unapprehended.

Because those [other than the *śrāvaka*s and bodhisattvas] have never cut off the roots of attachment, their contemplation doesn't clearly distinguish the two graspings (i.e., grasper and grasped). There are two attachments. In order to break the notion that there is a real agent of grasping, [the sutra] says, "There is no knowledge." To break the notion that something can be grasped, [the sutra] says, "There is no attainment."

The two negations (i.e., no knowledge and no attainment) can counteract both graspings. *No attachment* is to counteract the two graspings separately, for it breaks the notion of the existence of the grasped. *No knowledge* is to counteract the notion of the existence of subtle functions, for it eliminates the notion of the existence of the grasper.

This interpretation is to eradicate the attachment derived from mere imagination (*parikalpita*). The illusory phenomena (*shih*) of *paratantra* cannot be definitively [classified] as either "knowledge" or "attainment" (i.e., belonging to either grasper or grasped). Suchness is essentially tranquil and devoid of the two characteristics [of knowledge and attainment]. Therefore, according to the three natures, it is said there is no knowledge and no attainment. That which does not arise from true cognition (*chih; jñāna*) is not existent. Cognition and its object-sphere are called *prajñā,* since if there is no mark of grasping, there is no grasping of marks.

SUTRA: THEREFORE, BECAUSE OF NON-ATTAINMENT,

Commentary: The Madhyamikans comment that although the previous section [of the sutra], which states "In emptiness there is no form," concludes that form is not different from emptiness and is devoid of production and extinction, it does not explain the reason why form and so forth are nonexistent. Now, this passage reveals why there are no dharmas in emptiness. If the substance of form exists even slightly, according to ultimate truth, there will be some attainment. Since there is no attainment at all, originally all are empty. As the *Mahāprajñāpāramitā-sūtra* says, "Because the self-nature is empty, all are empty."

The Yogācārins comment that the *Madhyāntavibhāga*[-*śāstra*] says that a bodhisattva primarily practices ten [types of] skillful contemplations on: (1) the *skandhas*; (2) the sense fields; (3) the [eighteen] realms; (4) the dependent arisings; (5) the abodes and non-abodes; (6) the sense organs; (7) the world; (8) the truths; (9) the vehicles; and (10) the conditioned and unconditioned. Because Śāriputra was gradually awakened to the Mahayana, the sutra does not mention the six characteristics of the three vehicles, namely: the general, the particular, the close, the distant, the intensified,

and the fundamental practices. Through the two true contemplations, one realizes the noumenal and phenomenal aspects of the Dharma. These six characteristics that are grasped are nonexistent. The dharmas of dependent and consummate natures are definitely not of the six characteristics. Therefore, *non-attainment*
541a is used to explain the nonexistence [of the dharmas mentioned above]. The *Mahāprajñāpāramitā-sūtra* says, "Form and other dharmas are nonattainable, so is profound wisdom (*prajñā*)."

SUTRA: THE BODHISATTVA, HAVING RELIED ON THE PERFECTION OF WISDOM, ABIDES WITHOUT MENTAL OBSTRUCTIONS. BECAUSE OF THE NONEXISTENCE OF MENTAL OBSTRUCTIONS, HE HAS NO FEAR, HAS OVERCOME ALL PERVERTED VIEWS, HAS LEFT DREAMLIKE THOUGHTS FAR BEHIND, AND IN THE END ACHIEVES NIRVANA.

Commentary: The Madhyamikans comment that the first part of this passage refutes two kinds of attachment and broadly expounds two kinds of emptiness. The second part praises two kinds of reliance through which two kinds of benefit are obtained; that is, praising causal reliance, which severs obstructive defilements, and praising beneficial reliance, which is another name for the practices expounded previously.

Kua means obstruction, and *ai* means restrain. *K'ung* means fear, and *pu* means timidity. If one does not rely on wisdom, one will be obstructed by the impediments of form and so forth, and will sicken in suffering and fear. Due to this suffering and fear from the obstructions of illusory thought and samsara, one brings forth the aspiration for ultimate nirvana. By relying on wisdom through which one realizes that form is emptiness, one will be free from hindrance, suffering, fear, and mental obstructions. Because form and samsara are nothing but nirvana, why seek illusorily for ultimate nirvana? Therefore, by relying on wisdom, one leaves behind all [erroneous views].

The Yogācārins comment that the next passage [of the text] indicates that one leaves behind suffering and achieves perfect realization by relying on virtue and superior benefits to others.

This passage is to praise the benefits derived from the practices in the bodhisattva's causal stage. The bodhisattva constantly elucidates the literary meaning [of *prajñā*], trains to contemplate and meditate on the true form [of *prajñā*], and cultivates *prajñā* with a retinue. He does not seek illusorily to know all external phenomena. This is what is meant by "having relied on the perfection of wisdom."

Kua refers to the obstruction of the afflictions (*kleśāvaraṇa*), which prevents one from reaching nirvana; *ai* refers to the obstruction of the known (*jñeyāvaraṇa*), which prevents one from attaining enlightenment. Or, it may be said that *kua* is *ai,* for both denote the two obstructions [of affliction and of the known]. *Fear* is of five kinds: (1) fear of mortality, arising from the craving for one's existence; (2) fear of infamy, arising from not benefiting others and from having desires; (3) fear of death, arising from having the thought of the destruction of one's self; (4) fear of evil transmigrations, arising from not meeting with the Buddhas and from evil karma; and (5) fear of others, arising from seeing oneself as inferior and others as superior.

Perverted views (*viparyāsa*) refers to seven wrong notions. They are those of: (1) conceptualization (*saṃjñā*); (2) views (*dṛṣṭi*); (3) mind (*citta*); (4) seeing permanence in the impermanent; (5) seeing pleasure in suffering; (6) seeing purity in impurity; and (7) seeing the self in the selfless. The last four kinds of erroneous conceptual discriminations are called "conceptual perversions." Agreement with, longing for, building up, and attachment to desires are called "perverted views." Mental perversions are *kleśa*s which include three kinds: (1) the fundamental, referring to stupidity and doubt; (2) the substantial, referring to extremely one-sided views, heterodox ascetic views, views one desires and grasps, and views of a real self (*satkāyadṛṣṭi*); and (3) flow of the same type (*niṣyanda*), which refers to all other kinds of afflictions.

Dreamlike thoughts means that one is not really awakened to wisdom and thus is as if always abiding in a dream. Because of this, the Buddha said that samsara is like a long night. Dreams

are caused by thought, so they are called "dreamlike thought." The seven perverted views mentioned above are caused by erroneous thought. To act as if in a dream is called "dreamlike thought." Or, it can be explained that the perverted views mentioned above are
541b the causes of samsara and that dreamlike thought is the result of samsara, which is like the many bodies and objects seen in dreams; therefore the result [of samsara] indicates dreamlike thought.

Nirvana means perfect cessation (*yuan-chi*). Its substance pervades universally and its nature is profound. It accords with the nature of suchness, which is nondual and nondiscriminative. According to the realization of the cessation of the conditioned, there are four kinds of nirvana: (1) nirvana that is pure in its essential nature, referring to the real mark of the suchness of all dharmas; (2) non-abiding nirvana that is pure suchness, which is always assisted by great compassion and wisdom, and which transcends the obstruction of the known (*jñeyāvaraṇa*); (3) nirvana with remainder, referring to the suchness revealed after the cessation of the cause [of suffering]; and (4) nirvana without remainder, referring to the suchness revealed after the cessation of suffering.

As for the first kind of nirvana, it is commonly possessed by both ordinary people and holy ones, for all sentient beings have no birth and death and are originally in nirvana. As to the second kind [of nirvana], the bodhisattva abides in the [nirvana of] non-abiding. The *śrāvaka*s cannot attain this kind of nirvana. With regard to the last two kinds of nirvana, all those of the three vehicles can obtain liberation.

In summary, relying on the perfection of wisdom, the bodhisattva is awakened to the three non-natures and the emptiness of all things manifested through the two emptinesses of self and dharmas. His mind is not obstructed by the two kinds of hindrance, not disturbed by the five kinds of fear, not bound by the seven perverted views, and not deluded by the obstructions of dreamlike thoughts. He can ultimately realize nirvana.

Or, [it may be explained that] by relying on *prajñā*[-*pāramitā*], the bodhisattva, in the stage of superb understanding in the path of provisioning, gradually subdues discrimination of the two obstructions present before him. In the stage of intensified effort, he can either suddenly or gradually subdue the two inherent obstructions. His mind is free from hindrances. In the stage of the path of vision, he can then eliminate discrimination and attachment. His aspirations are fulfilled and he has no fear. In the stage of the path of cultivation, he increases his understanding and practice, cuts off all perverted views, and detaches from the dreamlike thoughts of birth and death. In the stage of no more to learn, he [realizes] ultimate nirvana, since what he practiced in the previous four stages has progressed [to this point].

In the abode of ultimate joy, all the afflictions of the evil destinies and the obstructions of the known, which are as coarse as skin, are eliminated forever. All afflictions (*kleśa*s) no longer appear and the mind is free from obstructions, for [the bodhisattva] has attained uncontaminated wisdom. In the abode of formless effortlessness, [the bodhisattva] cuts off forever all afflictions (*kleśa*s) that obstruct the wisdom of no-birth and the obstruction of the known, the crude barriers that were skin-deep. Because no *kleśa* appears, the bodhisattva has no fear. The cause is followed by the result, and in the resultant stage, all [fears] are severed. In the abode of ultimate fulfillment, [the bodhisattva] eliminates forever all *kleśa*s, karmic habits (*vāsanā*), proclivities (*anuśaya*), and the obstruction of the known, which were the crude barriers [at the level of] his bones. After entering the abode of the Tathāgatas, [the bodhisattva] leaves behind perverted views and dreamlike thoughts. Since the two kinds of obstruction have been eliminated in the three abodes, the bodhisattva has reached Buddhahood, final nirvana.

> SUTRA: ALL BUDDHAS OF THE THREE PERIODS OF TIME, AFTER RELYING ON THE PERFECTION OF WISDOM, REALIZE UNSURPASSED, RIGHT, COMPLETE ENLIGHTENMENT (*ANUTTARĀ-SAMYAK-SAṂBODHI*). 541c

Commentary: The Madhyamikans comment that the previous passage praises the cessation of the obstructions and the defiled benefits in the causal stage, and that this passage praises the attainment of *bodhi* benefits in the resultant stage. *Three periods of time* (*san-shih*) means past, present, and future. *All Buddhas* means not only one Buddha. The Sanskrit word *buddha* is abbreviated as *fo,* meaning "lord of wisdom." The Chinese translation of Buddha is *Chueh-che* ("Enlightened One"). *Te* means to realize. *A* (*an*) denotes negation. *Nou-tou-luo* (*uttarā*) means nothing goes beyond. *Sam* (*sam*) means right. *Miao* (*yak*) means complete. *Saṃ* again means right. *P'u-t'i* (*bodhi*) means enlightenment. *Mārga* means path; it is omitted in the text. *Unsurpassed* (*anuttarā*) means not surpassed. To know completely the noumenal and phenomenal is what is meant by *right* and *complete.* To leave behind the false and to illuminate the true is called "right enlightenment." Thus *anuttarā-samyak-saṃbodhi* means nothing-beyond, right, complete enlightenment.

The *Mahāprajñāpāramitā-śāstra* (*Ta-chih-tu-lun*) says that [both] wisdom [itself] and the object of wisdom are called "*prajñā.*" The enlightened ones of the past, present, and future have all relied on it. To realize right enlightenment is to realize wisdom and comprehend emptiness. Or, [it may be explained that] the nature of emptiness is enlightenment and that the subtle substance of the Tathāgata is the *dharmakāya*.

The Yogācārins comment that to transcend samsara and to awaken to wisdom is likened to waking from a dream. To tally with the nature of the Dharma, and to explain it, is likened to the blossoming of a flower. After attaining true and conventional wisdom, accomplishing enlightenment for oneself and others, and perfecting knowledge and practice, one is called a "Buddha." [Although a Buddha] does not need further practice after the perfection of enlightenment, he does not forsake [the practice] of helping sentient beings. Therefore, it is said, "The Buddhas have relied on *prajñā.*" Reliance can also denote [the results of prior] practice. In other words, in the causal stage the Buddhas have relied on the practice of *prajñā* and thus have attained complete enlightenment.

This reveals five characteristics. The pure Dharma realm, which is the Buddha's *dharmakāya,* suchness, and nirvana, possesses truly wonderful merits and results from contemplating the principle of emptiness. The other four kinds of wisdom refer to conditioned qualities, that is, the fruition of realized *saṃbhogakāya,* which results from the practice of self-benefit. The pure and magnificent Buddha body that manifests for the Mahābodhisattvas (Great Bodhisattvas) is called the "*saṃbhogakāya* for others' benefit." The Buddha body that manifests undeterminedly, either in a pure or defiled form, for those of the two vehicles is called the "*nirmāṇakāya.*" Both bodies appear in response to others' needs in order to benefit them.

The "*saṃbhogakāya* for own enjoyment" possesses one hundred forty uncommon qualities, such as the Tathāgata's thirty-two marks of a great person; the eighty subtle characteristics; the four kinds of purity; the ten powers; the four fearlessnesses; the three mindfulnesses (*tri-smṛtyupasthānāna*); great compassion; never forgetting the Dharma; permanent severance of habit; all types of subtle wisdom; the eight liberations; the eight stages in meditation; the *samādhi*s of nine degrees; the ten universals [of contemplating the universe from ten aspects]; the four immeasurables; the three emancipations; the three kinds of realization of no rebirth; the thirty-seven dharmas [factors] leading to *bodhi;* the five eyes; the six supernatural powers; the four unobstructed understandings; wisdom from the vow of being non-disputatious; constantly dwelling in equanimity; the eighteen uncommon characteristics of a Buddha, 542a
and so forth, up to omniscience (*sarvajñā*) and immeasurable qualities which are too many to mention.

The "*saṃbhogakāya* for others" and the *nirmāṇakāya* also have similar qualities. The conditioned qualities are subsumed under the four kinds of wisdom. Wisdom is the core of *bodhi-jñāna* (knowledge of enlightenment). The suchness of the *dharmakāya* is called the *bodhi* that cuts off [afflictions]. A sutra says that both *bodhi-jñāna* and the *bodhi* that cuts off [afflictions] are generally called "*bodhi.*" Thus, those who know *bodhi* are provisionally called Buddhas, which, in general, is a heuristic for realizing and attaining the special Dharma. Hence [the sutra] says that Buddhas attain *bodhi,* which includes exhaustive qualities. Wisdom that cuts off [the obstructions] and is perfectly fulfilled is called "unsurpassed awakening." The knowledge of ordinary people can only be called "right enlightenment." The partial wisdom of those of the two vehicles can only be called "equal enlightenment." The incomplete wisdom of the bodhisattva can only be called "right enlightenment." Only the perfect realization of the Buddha can be called "unsurpassed, right, complete enlightenment" (*anuttarā-samyak-saṃbodhi*).

The *Vajracchedikā-prajñāpāramitā-sūtra* says that all Buddhas and all Tathāgatas are born from this sutra. Therefore, the three bodies of the Buddha are all *bodhi*. The *Adhyardhaśatikā-sūtra* says that one who has faith in and studies this sutra can quickly fulfill bodhisattva practices and immediately realize unsurpassed, right, complete enlightenment. Therefore, *saṃbodhi* is attained through this (*prajñāpāramitā*).

> SUTRA: THEREFORE, ONE SHOULD KNOW *PRAJÑĀPĀRAMITĀ* AS THE GREAT MARVELOUS MANTRA, THE GREAT ILLUMINATING MANTRA, THE UNSURPASSED MANTRA, THE UNEQUALED MANTRA

Commentary: The Madhyamikans comment that the previous passage has already separately expounded the two causal reliances and the two resultant benefits. This passage summarizes and praises the supreme function of *prajñā*. To continue from the previous passage to the next, [the phrase] *therefore, one should know* is used.

Shen means marvelous, unlimited function. *Illuminating* (*ming*) means shining through all darkness. *Unsurpassed* (*wu-shang*) means the utmost. *Unequaled* (*wu-teng-teng*) means incomparable. The Great Master's (i.e., the Buddha) secret Dharma reveals the orthodox, destroys the heterodox, eliminates evil, and attends to goodness. It is respected and followed by spirits and holy ones. Its great power is beyond measure and is therefore called a "mantra."

The Yogācārins commented that the Sanskrit word *dhāraṇī* was translated [in Chinese] as *tsung-ch'ih*. Briefly there are four kinds: (1) Dharma [*dhāraṇī*,] which encompasses the comprehensive [Dharma]

in a condensed [mantra]; (2) meaning of [*dhāraṇī*,] which encompasses the comprehensive meaning [of the Dharma] through the concise meaning [of the mantra]; (3) the *dhāraṇī* that is able to cause a bodhisattva to attain the belief in no rebirth. Maitreya Bodhisattva said, "*Yi-t'i-mi-t'i-chi-t'i-p'i-ch'an-t'i po-t'o-ni sha-ho*"; (4) mantra—in the *Mahāprajñāpāramitā-sūtra* this mantra is found: *Na-mu-po-ch'ieh-fa-ti po-la-huai po-lo-mi-to-i tan chih-t'a shih-shai-i shih-shai-i shih-shai-i shih-shai-i hsi-sha-ho* (*Namo bhagavate prajñāpāramitāye tadyathā śriye śriye śriyase svāhā*). The extraordinary power of this mantra is extensively expounded in sutras. The mantra is comprised of recollection, wisdom, and myriads of qualities. According to the old tradition, [*dhāraṇi*] is generally called 542b
"mantra." The previous section of the sutra elucidates the essential meaning, while this section teaches a mantra.

From the mantra come forth the four categories of *sentient beings:* common people, *śrāvaka*s, *pratyekabuddha*s, and bodhisattvas. [From the mantra comes forth] the marvelous function of the text and terms; the perfect illumination of the contemplative [*prajñā*], the superior beneficial [*prajñā* with a] retinue, the incomparable true form [of *prajñā*], or all four aspects [of *prajñā*]. Therefore, *prajñā* is called "the great marvelous mantra" and so forth, up to the "unsurpassed mantra."

To exhort learners to practice the ten practices according to this sutra, Maitreya spoke this verse:

> Copying [scriptures], making offerings,
> Giving to others, listening [to others' recitations], reading
> [sutras],
> Upholding [the Dharma], explaining to others,
> Reciting, pondering, and putting into practice;
>
> One who cultivates these ten practices
> Attains immeasurable blessings.
> [These ten practices are] superior and inexhaustible,
> Because they never cease benefiting beings.

SUTRA: WHICH ELIMINATES ALL SUFFERING.

Commentary: The previous passage indicates the qualities [of the mantra], and this passage indicates that it can destroy evil. To have faith in, learn, realize, and expound it can eliminate suffering. Therefore, the *Mahāprajñāpāramitā-sūtra* says that one who practices the ten practices with regard to this sutra will not be tainted by any obstacles. Although one might create the most seriously vicious karma, one can get away from all evil destinies. Even if one had killed all beings in the three realms, one would never fall into the destinies of the hell beings, animals, or hungry ghosts. [Even] if one abides in all kinds of afflictions, one is like a lotus flower untainted by mud. One always comes together with all good things and attains unobstructed wisdom with regard to the Dharma and beings. One can skillfully comprehend the nature of equanimity and subdue one's own and others' anger. To one's present enemies, one brings forth compassionate thoughts. One can always see the Buddhas, attain the power to know all previous transmigrations, and remember the true Dharma one has heard.

All kinds of joy and happiness frequently manifest before oneself. One is always vigorous in practicing good dharmas; thus, no evil demons or heretics can linger and the four heavenly kings always accompany and protect [one]. One will never suffer a violent death nor encounter disasters. At all times, all Buddhas and bodhisattvas protect and help [one] to increase good and decrease evil. As one wishes, one can be born in any Buddha land one wishes. One does not fall into the evil destinies but swiftly fulfills all bodhisattva practices and quickly realizes unsurpassed, right, complete enlightenment (*anuttarā-samyak-saṃbodhi*). Regardless of what one wishes for, there is nothing that one cannot do. Hence, as soon as the four assemblies [of Buddhists] (i.e., monks, nuns, laymen, and laywomen), at the king's capital have recited [the mantra], all demons are subdued. As soon as it is upheld by Avalokiteśvara who has one thousand eyes, enmity disperses. How much more so [would benefits ensue] if a person deeply and sincerely cultivates the cause [of *bodhi*] and its perfect fruition? How could [such a person] not transcend the five paths of transmigration and become a master striding over the ten directions?

SUTRA: IT IS TRUE.

Commentary: This is repeated to eliminate doubt and to promote faith. How can the Holy One (the Buddha), who renounced 542c
the position of a *cakravartin,* who stayed in quiet woods, who gave up all his possessions, who was honored as a kind father and a Dharma king, who practiced all practices, who guided great sages and heavenly beings, deceive people? This is not possible. Therefore, this sutra states that the Tathāgata is one who speaks the truth and only the truth. So one should have faith and not give rise to alarm and doubt.

SUTRA: BY *PRAJÑĀPĀRAMITĀ* HAS THIS MANTRA BEEN DELIVERED. IT GOES LIKE THIS: GONE, GONE BEYOND, GONE ALTOGETHER BEYOND, OH! WHAT AN AWAKENING! ALL HAIL! (*GATE GATE PĀRAGATE PĀRASAṂGATE BODHI SVĀHĀ*)

Commentary: The doctrine and meaning expounded above is to exhort people to bring forth faith and to study, and in order to help them quickly get the essence, the mantra is taught. Because wisdom and compassion are difficult to practice in the era of the great *kalpa,* the Buddha vowed to employ concise words. The intention [of the mantra] is profound and its doctrine abstruse and broad. It is not easy to comment on it in detail.

Appendix

The *Heart Sutra* (*Prajñāpāramitā-hṛdaya-sūtra*)

Following is the complete text of the *Heart Sutra*, with page references for the commentary pertaining to each section.

Glossary

arhat: One who has freed himself from the bonds of birth and death by eliminating all passions. The highest spiritual ideal of the Hinayana. *See also* Hinayana.

Asaṅga: An early Indian Mahayana Buddhist teacher, who with his brother Vasubandhu founded the Yogācāra school. *See also* Mahayana; Vasubandhu; Yogacārā.

Avalokiteśvara: The bodhisattva who represents great compassion.

bhūmi: A stage or level of spiritual development. The ten *bhūmi*s are extensively elucidated in the *Avataṃsaka Sutra.*

bodhi: See enlightenment.

bodhisattva: A person who has experienced the profound aspiration to achieve perfect enlightenment (*bodhicitta*) on behalf of all sentient beings. Śākyamuni is referred to as the Bodhisattva prior to his attainment of Buddhahood, and his life forms the model emulated in Mahayana Buddhism. *See also* Mahayana; Śākyamuni.

Buddha-nature: The basic enlightened nature of sentient beings, which is chronically obscured by their ignorance. The complete unfolding of the Buddha-nature is enlightenment itself.

consciousness only (*vijñapti-mātra*): The central teaching of the Yogācāra school of Buddhism which indicates that we mistakenly take mental constructions (*vijñapti*) as presenting realities external to the consciousness (*vijñāna*) in which they appear. *See also* Yogācāra.

conventional truth. *See* ultimate truth.

dependent arising: The Buddhist doctrine that everything that exists comes into being in dependence on causes and conditions. Also called *pratītya-samutpāda.*

dhāraṇī: A special verbal formula that contains the essence of a teaching in short phrases and that is believed to hold great power. The original meanings are sometimes not known. Also called mantra.

dharmadhātu ("dharma realm"): Literally, the objects (dharmas) of the mind in general. It also means the entire universe, or the fundamental spiritual reality underlying all the illusions and things of the phenomenal world.

dharmakāya ("dharma body"): One of the three bodies, or manifestations, of a Buddha. The *dharmakāya* is the absolute or ultimate body of a Buddha, which is identical to ultimate truth or suchness. *See also nirmāṇakāya; saṃbhogakāya;* suchness; ultimate truth.

dhyāna: Meditation.

emptiness (*śūnyatā*): The fundamental teaching of Mahayana Buddhism, signifying the lack of *svabhāva,* or self-nature, inherent nature, independent being, self-defining essence, or invariant identity of anything. All phenomena (dharmas) occur only in dependence on causes and conditions. *See also* dependent arising; Mahayana; self-nature.

enlightenment (*bodhi*): The supreme wisdom, the state in which one is awakened to the true nature (suchness) of things. *See also* suchness.

five *skandhas* ("aggregates"): The five mental and physical factors of form, feeling, perception, impulses, and consciousness that collectively make up the "personality." According to Buddhism, a "person" or "being" is simply these five factors; there is no essential selfhood or inherent self-nature. *See also* self-nature.

Four Noble Truths: The basic teaching of the Buddha. They are: (1) Existence is characterized by suffering; (2) craving and attachment are the cause of suffering; (3) all suffering can be ended; (4) the way to end suffering is by following the Buddha's eightfold path (i.e., right view, right thought, right speech, right action, right livelihood, right effort, right mindfulness, and right concentration).

Hinayana ("Lesser Vehicle"): The name given by Mahayanists to early Buddhist teachings that had as their ideal the arhat; the two kinds of followers of this teaching, *śrāvaka*s and *pratyekabuddha*s, are known as followers of the two vehicles. *See also* arhat; Mahayana; *pratyekabuddha; śrāvaka.*

icchantika: A person who does not possess roots of goodness and therefore can never become a Buddha.

Jambudvīpa: The southern continent of the Buddhist cosmos, corresponding to our world.

jñeyāvaraṇa ("obstruction of the known"): The deeper of the two mental obstructions (*āvaraṇa*s), which involves adhering to ingrained erroneous views, especially the view of independent, inherent selfhood. *See also kleśāvaraṇa.*

kleśāvaraṇa ("obstruction of the afflictions"): The obstructions (*āvaraṇa*s), caused by unwholesome mental and emotional states such as desire, hatred, arrongance, etc., which are collectively known as "afflictions" (*kleśas*). *See also jñeyāvaraṇa.*

Madhyamika: One of the major Mahayana schools of Buddhism, established by Nāgārjuna and his followers. Its tenets are mainly based on the Prajñāpāramitā sutras, which stress the teaching of emptiness. *See also* emptiness; Nāgārjuna; Mahayana; Prajñāpāramitā.

Mahayana ("Great Vehicle"): A form of Buddhism that developed in India around 100 B.C.E. and which exalts as its religious ideal the bodhisattva, great beings who are willing to delay their own enlightenment until they can save all sentient beings. Such selfless compassion becomes possible only when the practitioner grasps the central Mahayana doctrine of emptiness and so realizes that "self" and "others" are not separate. *See also* bodhisattva; emptiness.

Maitreya: The future Buddha, currently still a bodhisattva.

Mañjuśrī: The bodhisattva who represents wisdom.

mantra. See *dhāraṇī.*

Nāgārjuna (ca. 150–250): An influential Mahayana teacher who established the Madhyamika school, which emphasized the doctrine of emptiness. He is acknowledged as founder by eight of the main Mahayana schools in the Buddhist tradition. *See also* emptiness; Madhyamika; Mahayana.

nirmāṇakāya ("transformation body"): One of the three bodies, or manifestations, of a Buddha. The *nirmāṇakāya* is an "incarnate" or "historically manifested" body of a Buddha, such as Śākyamuni, which appears in the world in order to guide sentient beings in a manner adapted to their situations and abilities. *See also dharmakāya;* Śākyamuni; *saṃbhogakāya.*

nirvana: The final goal of Buddhist aspiration and practice, a state in which passions are extinguished and the highest wisdom attained. Liberation from samsara. *See also* samsara.

one vehicle: A doctrine particularly emphasized in the *Lotus Sutra.* According to that sutra, the one vehicle is the ultimate teaching of the Buddha, although the Buddha taught three other types of teachings (i.e., the *śrāvaka* vehicle, the *pratyekabuddha* vehicle, and the bodhisattva vehicle) as skillful means to guide all sentient beings to the one vehicle. *See also* bodhisattva; *pratyekabuddha; śrāvaka.*

prajñā: Nondiscriminating or transcendental wisdom, the understanding of things in their actual realities. One of the six perfections (*pāramitā*s) of a bodhisattva. *See also* bodhisattva; six perfections.

Prajñāpāramitā ("perfection of wisdom"): The name of a body of Mahayana literature that emphasizes the doctrine of emptiness, and which served as fundamental texts for a number of Buddhist schools, including Madhyamika and Yogācāra. As a technical term, *prajñāpāramitā* refers to the perfection of wisdom accomplished by a bodhisattva on the way to perfect enlightenment. *See also* bodhisattva; emptiness; Madhyamika; Mahayana; six perfections; Yogācāra.

pratītyasamutpāda: See dependent arising.

pratyekabuddha: A sage who attains enlightenment by observing the principles of causation and dependent arising by himself. He attains emancipation without the guidance of a teacher, and he intends neither to guide others nor to expound the teaching to others. One of the two kinds of Hinayana sages. *See also* Hinayana; *śrāvaka.*

Śākyamuni: The historical Buddha who lived in India in the fifth century B.C.E., and whose life and teachings form the basis of Buddhism.

samādhi: A state of meditative concentration.

saṃbhogakāya ("enjoyment body"): One of the three bodies, or manifestations, of a Buddha. The *saṃbhogakāya* is a spiritual body which a Buddha assumes both as a reward for eons of practice and in order to expound the Dharma to bodhisattvas and others. *See also dharmakāya; nirmāṇakāya.*

samsara: The cycle of birth, death, and rebirth into the world of suffering. The Buddha's teachings are designed to lead sentient beings to liberation from the cycle of samsara, which is the state of nirvana. *See also* nirvana.

Śāriputra: One of the original disciples of the Buddha, called "foremost of the wise."

self-nature: The quality of having a permanent, unchanging existence independent of causes and conditions. Both the Madhyamika and the Yogācāra school hold that nothing really has this kind of independent, inherent self-nature. *See also* emptiness; Madhyamika; Yogācāra.

sense fields (*āyatana*): The six sense organs—eye, ear, nose, tongue, body, and mind—and their respective objects of perception. *See also* sense realms; six consciousnesses.

sense realms (*dhātu*): The eighteen sense realms are the six sense organs (i.e., eye, ear, nose, tongue, body, and mind), their six corresponding perceptual objects (i.e., sight object, hearing object, etc.), and the six corresponding forms of consciousness that arise on the basis of the contact between a sense organ and a sense object. *See also* sense fields; six consciousnesses.

six consciousnesses: (1) Eye consciousness (sight); (2) ear consciousness (hearing); (3) nose consciousness (smell); (4) tongue consciousness (taste); (5) body consciousness (touch); and (6) mind consciousness (the mental sense or intellect).

six perfections (*pāramitā*s): The six perfect virtues cultivated by a bodhisattva on the way to complete enlightenment. They are: (1) giving (*dāna*); (2) morality (*śīla*); (3) patience (*kṣānti*); (4) effort (*vīrya*); (5) concentration (*dhyāna*); and (6) wisdom (*prajñā*). *See also* bodhisattva.

śrāvaka: Originally, a disciple of the historical Buddha, one who directly heard his teachings. Later generally used to mean Hinayana Buddhists. *See also* Hinayana.

suchness (*tathatā*): The state of things as they really are; ultimate truth; ultimate reality. The content of the perfect wisdom (*prajñāpāramitā*) insight into the nature of reality just as it is, i.e., empty of self-nature and dependently arisen. Apprehension of this state is enlightenment. *See also* dependent arising; emptiness; enlightenment; Prajñāpāramitā; self-nature; ultimate truth.

Tathāgata: An epithet for the Buddha. It means "one who has gone to (*gata*) and come from (*āgata*) the truth of suchness (*tathā*)," i.e., "one who embodies the truth of suchness (*tathā*)." *See also* suchness.

tathāgatagarbha: Another name for the Buddha-nature that is within all beings. It is conceived of as a kind of storeroom or receptacle where the embryo of the Tathāgata is retained and matured. *See also* Buddha-nature; Tathāgata.

Three Jewels: The Buddha, the Dharma (the Buddha's teachings), and the Sangha (the community of his followers).

two vehicles. *See* Hinayana.

ultimate truth: The truth that is beyond words and conceptualization. It is generally contrasted with conventional truth, which can be expressed verbally and conceptualized but which is not reflective of suchness, or reality-as-it-is. *See also* suchness.

Vasubandhu: An early Indian Buddhist teacher and founder, with his brother Asaṅga, of the Yogācāra school. Born in Gandhāra in the fourth century, Vasubandhu was at first a Hinayana follower and wrote the *Abhidharmakośa*. He later converted to Mahayana Buddhism and wrote many important Yogācāra texts and treatises. *See also* Asaṅga; Mahayana; Yogācāra.

Yogacārā: A major Mahayana Buddhist philosophical school, founded in the fourth century by Asaṅga and Vasubandhu, which advocates the doctrine of "consciousness only." *See also* Asaṅga; consciousness only; Mahayana; Vasubandhu.

Bibliography

Conze, Edward, trans. *Buddhist Wisdom Books Containing the Diamond Sutra and the Heart Sutra*. London: Unwin Paperbacks, 1988.

Conze, Edward. "The *Prajñāpāramitā-hṛdaya Sūtra*." In *Thirty Years of Buddhist Studies: Selected Essays by Edward Conze*. Oxford: Bruno Cassirer, 1967.

Hariba, Gensui. *Hannya shingyō ihon taisei*. Tokyo: Yoyogi Shoten, 1932.

Hurvitz, Leon. "Hsuän-tsang (602–664) and the *Heart Scripture*." In *Prajñāpāramitā and Related Systems: Studies in Honor of Edward Conze*. Edited by Lewis Lancaster. Berkeley Buddhist Studies Series 1. Berkeley, CA: The Group in Buddhist Studies and the Center for South & Southeast Asian Studies, University of California, Berkeley, 1977.

Index

A

abiding 11, 19, 32, 33, 38, 39, 42, 43, 45, 49, 58, 61, 64, 69, 71–7, 86, 111, 117, 125
abode(s) (*see also bhūmi*) 20, 71–7, 79, 80, 81, 88, 96, 115, 119
  bodhisattva 71, 77
  of formless effortlessness 77, 81, 119
  seventh 77, 88
  of the Tathāgata(s) 71, 81, 88, 119
  thirteen 3, 71, 79, 80
  of ultimate joy 77, 81, 119
ādāna 104
Adhyardhaśatikā-sūtra 122
affliction(s) (*see also kleśa;* obstruction, of the afflictions) 7, 10, 13, 14, 18, 21, 22, 24, 39, 42, 46, 54, 56, 60, 63, 73, 77, 86, 88, 91, 106, 109, 112, 117, 119, 121, 124
aggregate(s) (*see also skandha*) 82, 96
ālambaka (*see also* cognitive conditions) 33, 104
ālambana (*see also* object-support) 16, 27, 29, 30, 32, 84, 104
ālaya-vijñāna (*see also* consciousness, eighth) 18, 104, 105
anāsrava (*see also* uncontaminated) 25, 33, 34, 104, 112
anuttarā-samyak-saṃbodhi (*see also bodhi;* enlightenment) 23, 119, 120, 122, 124, 127
arhat(s) 109
ārya. See sage
arūpadhātu. See three realms, formless
Asaṅga 9, 23
aspiration(s) 13, 14, 15, 16, 20, 21, 23, 31, 57, 61–2, 71, 89, 116, 119
  for enlightenment (*see also bodhicitta*) 11, 13, 19, 22, 23, 47, 51, 61, 62, 71, 78
ātman. See self
attachment(s) 1, 7, 8, 9, 12, 15, 17, 22, 32, 54, 59, 68, 82, 83, 84, 90, 94, 96, 98, 100, 101, 104, 106, 110, 111, 113, 114, 115, 117, 119
  to self 13, 63, 74, 84, 85, 97, 100, 104, 106
  two 85, 90, 95, 106, 114, 116
attainment (*see also* non-attainment) 12, 14, 23, 33, 35, 45, 53, 69, 73, 78, 81, 85, 102, 113, 114, 115, 120, 128
Avalokiteśvara (*see also* Kuan-tzu-tsai) 12, 13, 124, 127
Avataṃsaka-sūtra 25
āyatana(s) (*see also* sense field) 87, 90, 100, 101

B

barriers 88
  crude 87, 88, 119
  four 13, 89, 96
beneficial friends 7, 19, 21, 23, 45, 58–9, 61
bhūmi(s) (*see also* stage) 3, 12, 33, 65, 71–7, 79, 84, 88, 105, 110, 113
  eighth 33, 34, 75–6, 88
  fifth 33, 74, 113
  first 20, 33, 64, 67, 71, 72, 105
  fourth 74
  ninth 76
  second 72–3
  seven 79
  seventh 33, 34, 75, 88, 110
  sixth 75, 110, 113
  ten 20, 64, 65, 67, 68
  tenth 49, 67, 76–7, 84, 88
  third 73–4, 79
bīja(s). *See* seeds
"Biographical Study of Tz'u-en, A" 2
birth (*see also* destinies; no-birth; rebirth) 14, 19, 35, 62, 66, 72, 76, 78, 86, 87, 107, 108, 109, 110
  and death (*see also* cyclic existtence; samsara) 14, 15, 16, 51, 88, 106, 110, 112, 118, 119
  five kinds of 77–8
  four kinds of 35
  transformational 102, 103
bodhi (*see also anuttarā-samyaksaṃbodhi;* enlightenment) 11, 14, 15, 34, 36, 96, 97, 110, 114, 120, 121, 122, 124, 125, 128
bodhicitta (*see also* aspiration, toward enlightenment) 11, 19, 20, 21, 23, 61, 71
bodhisattva(s) 3, 11, 12, 13, 14, 15, 19, 21, 23, 26, 32, 33, 34, 36, 37, 42, 47, 48, 55, 59, 61, 62, 65, 66, 67, 68, 69, 71, 72, 73, 74, 75, 76, 77, 78, 79, 80, 81, 83, 84, 85, 86, 88, 92, 93, 99, 100, 101, 110, 111, 113, 114, 115, 116, 117, 118, 119, 121, 122, 123, 124, 127, 128
  stages. *See* stage; *bhūmi*
Brahma 73
Brahma Heaven 57, 73
brahman(s) 78
Buddha (*see also* Śākyamuni; World-honored One) 7, 8, 9, 10, 12, 17, 19, 22, 23, 25, 26, 32, 35, 37, 38, 47, 48, 53, 57, 62, 64, 72, 73, 75, 76, 77, 78, 80, 82, 83, 89, 92, 100, 101, 103, 105, 106, 109, 110, 113, 117, 120, 121, 122, 125
Buddhas 8, 19, 21, 23, 24, 25, 26, 36, 37, 42, 49, 56, 57, 62, 67, 72, 117, 119, 120, 121, 122, 124, 128
Buddha body(ies) (*see also dharmakāya; nirmāṇakāya; saṃbhogakāya*) 20, 121, 122
Buddha-Dharma (*see also* Dharma; Holy Teaching) 21, 36, 41, 48, 50, 55, 74, 85
Buddhahood 11, 14, 20, 36, 78, 81, 105, 119
Buddha land(s) 62, 72, 124
Buddha-nature 31
Buddhism 2, 18
Buddhist(s) 1, 2, 40, 44, 48, 55, 72, 88, 124

C

N

R

S

T

A List of the Volumes of the BDK English Tripiṭaka (First Series)

Abbreviations

Ch.:	Chinese
Skt.:	Sanskrit
Jp.:	Japanese
Eng.:	Published title
T.:	Taishō Tripiṭaka

Vol. No.		Title	*T.* No.
1, 2	*Ch.*	Ch'ang-a-han-ching （長阿含經）	1
	Skt.	Dīrghāgama	
3–8	*Ch.*	Chung-a-han-ching （中阿含經）	26
	Skt.	Madhyamāgama	
9-I	*Ch.*	Ta-ch'eng-pên-shêng-hsin-ti-kuan-ching （大乘本生心地觀經）	159
9-II	*Ch.*	Fo-so-hsing-tsan （佛所行讃）	192
	Skt.	Buddhacarita	
10-I	*Ch.*	Tsa-pao-ts'ang-ching （雜寶藏經）	203
	Eng.	The Storehouse of Sundry Valuables	
10-II	*Ch.*	Fa-chü-p'i-yü-ching （法句譬喩經）	211
	Eng.	The Scriptural Text: Verses of the Doctrine, with Parables	
11-I	*Ch.*	Hsiao-p'in-pan-jo-po-lo-mi-ching （小品般若波羅蜜經）	227
	Skt.	Aṣṭasāhasrikā-prajñāpāramitā-sūtra	
11-II	*Ch.*	Chin-kang-pan-jo-po-lo-mi-ching （金剛般若波羅蜜經）	235
	Skt.	Vajracchedikā-prajñāpāramitā-sūtra	

Vol. No.		Title	*T.* No.
11-III	*Ch.*	Jên-wang-pan-jo-po-lo-mi-ching (仁王般若波羅蜜經)	245
	Skt.	Kāruṇikārājā-prajñāpāramitā-sūtra (?)	
11-IV	*Ch.*	Pan-jo-po-lo-mi-to-hsing-ching (般若波羅蜜多心經)	251
	Skt.	Prajñāpāramitāhṛdaya-sūtra	
12-I	*Ch.*	Ta-lo-chin-kang-pu-k'ung-chên-shih-san-mo-yeh-ching (大樂金剛不空眞實三麼耶經)	243
	Skt.	Adhyardhaśatikā-prajñāpāramitā-sūtra	
12-II	*Ch.*	Wu-liang-shou-ching (無量壽經)	360
	Skt.	Sukhāvatīvyūha	
	Eng.	The Larger Sutra on Amitāyus (In The Three Pure Land Sutras)	
12-III	*Ch.*	Kuan-wu-liang-shou-fo-ching (觀無量壽佛經)	365
	Skt.	Amitāyurdhyāna-sūtra	
	Eng.	The Sutra on Contemplation of Amitāyus (In The Three Pure Land Sutras)	
12-IV	*Ch.*	A-mi-t'o-ching (阿彌陀經)	366
	Skt.	Sukhāvatīvyūha	
	Eng.	The Smaller Sutra on Amitāyus (In The Three Pure Land Sutras)	
12-V	*Ch.*	Ti-ts'ang-p'u-sa-pên-yüan-ching (地藏菩薩本願經)	412
	Skt.	Kṣitigarbhapraṇidhāna-sūtra (?)	
12-VI	*Ch.*	Yao-shih-liu-li-kuang-ju-lai-pên-yüan-kung-tê-ching (藥師琉璃光如來本願功德經)	450
	Skt.	Bhaiṣajyaguruvaiḍūryaprabhāsapūrva-praṇidhānaviśeṣavistara	
12-VII	*Ch.*	Mi-lê-hsia-shêng-ch'êng-fo-ching (彌勒下生成佛經)	454
	Skt.	Maitreyavyākaraṇa (?)	
12-VIII	*Ch.*	Wên-shu-shih-li-wên-ching (文殊師利問經)	468
	Skt.	Mañjuśrīparipṛcchā (?)	
13-I	*Ch.*	Miao-fa-lien-hua-ching (妙法蓮華經)	262
	Skt.	Saddharmapuṇḍarīka-sūtra	
	Eng.	The Lotus Sutra	
13-II	*Ch.*	Wu-liang-i-ching (無量義經)	276

Vol. No.		Title	*T.* No.
13-III	*Ch.*	Kuan-p'u-hsien-p'u-sa-hsing-fa-ching (觀普賢菩薩行法經)	277
14–19	*Ch.*	Ta-fang-kuang-fo-hua-yen-ching (大方廣佛華嚴經)	278
	Skt.	Avataṃsaka-sūtra	
20-I	*Ch.*	Shêng-man-shih-tzŭ-hou-i-ch'eng-ta-fang-pien-fang-kuang-ching (勝鬘師子吼一乘大方便方廣經)	353
	Skt.	Śrīmālādevīsiṃhanāda-sūtra	
20-II	*Ch.*	Chin-kuang-ming-tsui-shêng-wang-ching (金光明最勝王經)	665
	Skt.	Suvarṇaprabhāsa-sūtra	
21–24	*Ch.*	Ta-pan-nieh-p'an-ching (大般涅槃經)	374
	Skt.	Mahāparinirvāṇa-sūtra	
25-I	*Ch.*	Fo-ch'ui-pan-nieh-p'an-liao-shuo-chiao-chieh-ching (佛垂般涅槃略説教誡經)	389
25-II	*Ch.*	Pan-chou-san-mei-ching (般舟三昧經)	418
	Skt.	Pratyutpannabuddhasammukhāvasthitasamādhi-sūtra	
	Eng.	The Pratyutpanna Samādhi Sutra	
25-III	*Ch.*	Shou-lêng-yen-san-mei-ching (首楞嚴三昧經)	642
	Skt.	Śūraṅgamasamādhi-sūtra	
	Eng.	The Śūraṅgama Samādhi Sutra	
25-IV	*Ch.*	Chieh-shên-mi-ching (解深密經)	676
	Skt.	Saṃdhinirmocana-sūtra	
	Eng.	The Scripture on the Explication of Underlying Meaning	
25-V	*Ch.*	Yü-lan-p'ên-ching (盂蘭盆經)	685
	Skt.	Ullambana-sūtra (?)	
25-VI	*Ch.*	Ssŭ-shih-êrh-chang-ching (四十二章經)	784
26-I	*Ch.*	Wei-mo-chieh-so-shuo-ching (維摩詰所説經)	475
	Skt.	Vimalakīrtinirdeśa-sūtra	
26-II	*Ch.*	Yüeh-shang-nü-ching (月上女經)	480
	Skt.	Candrottarādārikāparipṛcchā	

Vol. No.		**Title**	***T.* No.**
26-III	*Ch.*	Tso-ch'an-san-mei-ching (坐禪三昧經)	614
26-IV	*Ch.*	Ta-mo-to-lo-ch'an-ching (達磨多羅禪經)	618
	Skt.	Yogācārabhūmi-sūtra (?)	
27	*Ch.*	Yüeh-têng-san-mei-ching (月燈三昧經)	639
	Skt.	Samādhirājacandrapradīpa-sūtra	
28	*Ch.*	Ju-lêng-ch'ieh-ching (入楞伽經)	671
	Skt.	Laṅkāvatāra-sūtra	
29-I	*Ch.*	Ta-fang-kuang-yüan-chio-hsiu-to-lo-liao-i-ching (大方廣圓覺修多羅了義經)	842
29-II	*Ch.*	Su-hsi-ti-chieh-lo-ching (蘇悉地羯囉經)	893
	Skt.	Susiddhikaramahātantrasādhanopāyika-paṭala	
29-III	*Ch.*	Mo-têng-ch'ieh-ching (摩登伽經)	1300
	Skt.	Mātaṅgī-sūtra (?)	
30-I	*Ch.*	Ta-p'i-lu-chê-na-chêng-fo-shên-pien-chia-ch'ih-ching (大毘盧遮那成佛神變加持經)	848
	Skt.	Mahāvairocanābhisambodhivikurvitādhiṣṭhāna-vaipulyasūtrendrarāja-nāma-dharmaparyāya	
30-II	*Ch.*	Ching-kang-ting-i-ch'ieh-ju-lai-chên-shih-shê-ta-ch'eng-hsien-chêng-ta-chiao-wang-ching (金剛頂一切如來眞實攝大乘現證大教王經)	865
	Skt.	Sarvatathāgatatattvasaṃgrahamahāyānābhi-samayamahākalparāja	
31–35	*Ch.*	Mo-ho-sêng-ch'i-lü (摩訶僧祇律)	1425
	Skt.	Mahāsāṃghika-vinaya (?)	
36–42	*Ch.*	Ssŭ-fên-lü (四分律)	1428
	Skt.	Dharmaguptaka-vinaya (?)	
43, 44	*Ch.*	Shan-chien-lü-p'i-p'o-sha (善見律毘婆沙)	1462
	Pāli	Samantapāsādikā	
45-I	*Ch.*	Fan-wang-ching (梵網經)	1484
	Skt.	Brahmajāla-sūtra (?)	
45-II	*Ch.*	Yu-p'o-sai-chieh-ching (優婆塞戒經)	1488
	Skt.	Upāsakaśīla-sūtra (?)	
	Eng.	The Sutra on Upāsaka Precepts	

Vol. No.		Title	*T.* No.
46-I	*Ch.*	Miao-fa-lien-hua-ching-yu-po-t'i-shê (妙法蓮華經憂波提舍)	1519
	Skt.	Saddharmapuṇḍarīka-upadeśa	
46-II	*Ch.*	Fo-ti-ching-lun (佛地經論)	1530
	Skt.	Buddhabhūmisūtra-śāstra (?)	
46-III	*Ch.*	Shê-ta-ch'eng-lun (攝大乘論)	1593
	Skt.	Mahāyānasaṃgraha	
	Eng.	The Summary of the Great Vehicle	
47	*Ch.*	Shih-chu-p'i-p'o-sha-lun (十住毘婆沙論)	1521
	Skt.	Daśabhūmika-vibhāṣā (?)	
48, 49	*Ch.*	A-p'i-ta-mo-chü-shê-lun (阿毘達磨倶舍論)	1558
	Skt.	Abhidharmakośa-bhāṣya	
50–59	*Ch.*	Yü-ch'ieh-shih-ti-lun (瑜伽師地論)	1579
	Skt.	Yogācārabhūmi	
60-I	*Ch.*	Ch'êng-wei-shih-lun (成唯識論)	1585
	Eng.	Demonstration of Consciousness Only (In Three Texts on Consciousness Only)	
60-II	*Ch.*	Wei-shih-san-shih-lun-sung (唯識三十論頌)	1586
	Skt.	Triṃśikā	
	Eng.	The Thirty Verses on Consciousness Only (In Three Texts on Consciousness Only)	
60-III	*Ch.*	Wei-shih-êrh-shih-lun (唯識二十論)	1590
	Skt.	Viṃśatikā	
	Eng.	The Treatise in Twenty Verses on Consciousness Only (In Three Texts on Consciousness Only)	
61-I	*Ch.*	Chung-lun (中論)	1564
	Skt.	Madhyamaka-śāstra	
61-II	*Ch.*	Pien-chung-pien-lun (辯中邊論)	1600
	Skt.	Madhyāntavibhāga	
61-III	*Ch.*	Ta-ch'eng-ch'êng-yeh-lun (大乘成業論)	1609
	Skt.	Karmasiddhiprakaraṇa	
61-IV	*Ch.*	Yin-ming-ju-chêng-li-lun (因明入正理論)	1630
	Skt.	Nyāyapraveśa	

Vol. No.		Title	*T.* No.
61-V	*Ch.*	Chin-kang-chên-lun （金剛針論）	1642
	Skt.	Vajrasūcī	
61-VI	*Ch.*	Chang-so-chih-lun （彰所知論）	1645
62	*Ch.*	Ta-ch'eng-chuang-yen-ching-lun（大乘莊嚴經論）	1604
	Skt.	Mahāyānasūtrālaṃkāra	
63-I	*Ch.*	Chiu-ching-i-ch'eng-pao-hsing-lun（究竟一乘寳性論）	1611
	Skt.	Ratnagotravibhāgamahāyānottaratantra-śāstra	
63-II	*Ch.*	P'u-t'i-hsing-ching （菩提行經）	1662
	Skt.	Bodhicaryāvatāra	
63-III	*Ch.*	Chin-kang-ting-yü-ch'ieh-chung-fa-a-nou-to-lo-san-miao-san-p'u-t'i-hsin-lun（金剛頂瑜伽中發阿耨多羅三藐三菩提心論）	1665
63-IV	*Ch.*	Ta-ch'eng-ch'i-hsin-lun （大乘起信論）	1666
	Skt.	Mahāyānaśraddhotpāda-śāstra (?)	
63-V	*Ch.*	Na-hsien-pi-ch'iu-ching （那先比丘經）	1670
	Pāli	Milindapañhā	
64	*Ch.*	Ta-ch'eng-chi-p'u-sa-hsüeh-lun（大乘集菩薩學論）	1636
	Skt.	Śikṣāsamuccaya	
65	*Ch.*	Shih-mo-ho-yen-lun （釋摩訶衍論）	1688
66-I	*Ch.*	Pan-jo-po-lo-mi-to-hsin-ching-yu-tsan（般若波羅蜜多心經幽賛）	1710
	Eng.	A Comprehensive Commentary on the Heart Sutra (Prajñāpāramitā-hṛdaya-sūtra)	
66-II	*Ch.*	Kuan-wu-liang-shou-fo-ching-shu（觀無量壽佛經疏）	1753
66-III	*Ch.*	San-lun-hsüan-i （三論玄義）	1852
66-IV	*Ch.*	Chao-lun （肇論）	1858
67, 68	*Ch.*	Miao-fa-lien-hua-ching-hsüan-i（妙法蓮華經玄義）	1716

Vol. No.		Title	*T.* No.
69	*Ch.*	Ta-ch'eng-hsüan-lun (大乘玄論)	1853
70-I	*Ch.*	Hua-yen-i-ch'eng-chiao-i-fên-ch'i-chang (華嚴一乘教義分齊章)	1866
70-II	*Ch.*	Yüan-jên-lun (原人論)	1886
70-III	*Ch.*	Hsiu-hsi-chih-kuan-tso-ch'an-fa-yao (修習止觀坐禪法要)	1915
70-IV	*Ch.*	T'ien-t'ai-ssŭ-chiao-i (天台四教儀)	1931
71, 72	*Ch.*	Mo-ho-chih-kuan (摩訶止觀)	1911
73-I	*Ch.*	Kuo-ch'ing-pai-lu (國清百録)	1934
73-II	*Ch.*	Liu-tsu-ta-shih-fa-pao-t'an-ching (六祖大師法寶壇經)	2008
	Eng.	The Platform Sutra of the Sixth Patriarch	
73-III	*Ch.*	Huang-po-shan-tuan-chi-ch'an-shih-ch'uan-hsin-fa-yao (黄檗山斷際禪師傳心法要)	2012A
73-IV	*Ch.*	Yung-chia-chêng-tao-ko (永嘉證道歌)	2014
74-I	*Ch.*	Chên-chou-lin-chi-hui-chao-ch'an-shih-wu-lu (鎭州臨濟慧照禪師語録)	1985
	Eng.	The Recorded Sayings of Linji (In Three Chan Classics)	
74-II	*Ch.*	Wu-mên-kuan (無門關)	2005
	Eng.	Wumen's Gate (In Three Chan Classics)	
74-III	*Ch.*	Hsin-hsin-ming (信心銘)	2010
	Eng.	The Faith-Mind Maxim (In Three Chan Classics)	
74-IV	*Ch.*	Ch'ih-hsiu-pai-chang-ch'ing-kuei (勅修百丈清規)	2025
75	*Ch.*	Fo-kuo-yüan-wu-ch'an-shih-pi-yen-lu (佛果圜悟禪師碧巖録)	2003
	Eng.	The Blue Cliff Record	
76-I	*Ch.*	I-pu-tsung-lun-lun (異部宗輪論)	2031
	Skt.	Samayabhedoparacanacakra	

Vol. No.		Title	*T.* No.
76-II	*Ch.* *Skt.* *Eng.*	A-yü-wang-ching （阿育王經） Aśokarāja-sūtra (?) The Biographical Scripture of King Aśoka	2043
76-III	*Ch.*	Ma-ming-p'u-sa-ch'uan （馬鳴菩薩傳）	2046
76-IV	*Ch.*	Lung-shu-p'u-sa-ch'uan （龍樹菩薩傳）	2047
76-V	*Ch.*	P'o-sou-p'an-tou-fa-shih-ch'uan （婆藪槃豆法師傳）	2049
76-VI	*Ch.*	Pi-ch'iu-ni-ch'uan （比丘尼傳）	2063 (7)
76-VII	*Ch.*	Kao-sêng-fa-hsien-ch'uan （高僧法顯傳）	2085
76-VIII	*Ch.*	Yu-fang-chi-ch'ao: T'ang-ta-ho-shang-tung-chêng-ch'uan（遊方記抄: 唐大和上東征傳）	2089-
77	*Ch.* *Eng.*	Ta-t'ang-ta-tz'ŭ-ên-ssŭ-san-ts'ang-fa-shih-ch'uan （大唐大慈恩寺三藏法師傳） A Biography of the Tripiṭaka Master of the Great Ci'en Monastery of the Great Tang Dynasty	2053
78	*Ch.*	Kao-sêng-ch'uan （高僧傳）	2059
79	*Ch.* *Eng.*	Ta-t'ang-hsi-yü-chi （大唐西域記） The Great Tang Dynasty Record of the Western Regions	2087
80	*Ch.*	Hung-ming-chi （弘明集）	2102
81–92	*Ch.*	Fa-yüan-chu-lin （法苑珠林）	2122
93-I	*Ch.* *Eng.*	Nan-hai-chi-kuei-nei-fa-ch'uan （南海寄歸内法傳） Buddhist Monastic Traditions of Southern Asia	2125
93-II	*Ch.*	Fan-yü-tsa-ming （梵語雜名）	2135
94-I	*Jp.*	Shō-man-gyō-gi-sho （勝鬘經義疏）	2185
94-II	*Jp.*	Yui-ma-kyō-gi-sho （維摩經義疏）	2186
95	*Jp.*	Hok-ke-gi-sho （法華義疏）	2187
96-I	*Jp.*	Han-nya-shin-gyō-hi-ken （般若心經秘鍵）	2203

Vol. No.		Title	*T.* No.
96-II	*Jp.*	Dai-jō-hos-sō-ken-jin-shō （大乘法相研神章）	2309
96-III	*Jp.*	Kan-jin-kaku-mu-shō （觀心覺夢鈔）	2312
97-I	*Jp.*	Ris-shū-kō-yō （律宗綱要）	2348
	Eng.	The Essentials of the Vinaya Tradition	
97-II	*Jp.*	Ten-dai-hok-ke-shū-gi-shū （天台法華宗義集）	2366
	Eng.	The Collected Teachings of the Tendai Lotus School	
97-III	*Jp.*	Ken-kai-ron （顯戒論）	2376
97-IV	*Jp.*	San-ge-gaku-shō-shiki （山家學生式）	2377
98-I	*Jp.*	Hi-zō-hō-yaku （秘藏寶鑰）	2426
98-II	*Jp.*	Ben-ken-mitsu-ni-kyō-ron （辨顯密二教論）	2427
98-III	*Jp.*	Soku-shin-jō-butsu-gi （即身成佛義）	2428
98-IV	*Jp.*	Shō-ji-jis-sō-gi （聲字實相義）	2429
98-V	*Jp.*	Un-ji-gi （吽字義）	2430
98-VI	*Jp.*	Go-rin-ku-ji-myō-hi-mitsu-shaku （五輪九字明秘密釋）	2514
98-VII	*Jp.*	Mitsu-gon-in-hotsu-ro-san-ge-mon （密嚴院發露懺悔文）	2527
98-VIII	*Jp.*	Kō-zen-go-koku-ron （興禪護國論）	2543
98-IX	*Jp.*	Fu-kan-za-zen-gi （普勧坐禪儀）	2580
99–103	*Jp.*	Shō-bō-gen-zō （正法眼藏）	2582
104-I	*Jp.*	Za-zen-yō-jin-ki （坐禪用心記）	2586
104-II	*Jp.*	Sen-chaku-hon-gan-nen-butsu-shū （選擇本願念佛集）	2608
	Eng.	Senchaku Hongan Nembutsu Shū	
104-III	*Jp.*	Ris-shō-an-koku-ron （立正安國論）	2688
104-IV	*Jp.*	Kai-moku-shō （開目抄）	2689
	Eng.	Kaimokushō or Liberation from Blindness	

Vol. No.		Title	*T.* No.
104-V	*Jp.*	Kan-jin-hon-zon-shō （觀心本尊抄）	2692
104-VI	*Ch.*	Fu-mu-ên-chung-ching （父母恩重經）	2887
105-I	*Jp.*	Ken-jō-do-shin-jitsu-kyō-gyō-shō-mon-rui （顯淨土眞實教行証文類）	2646
105-II	*Jp.*	Tan-ni-shō （歎異抄）	2661
	Eng.	Tannishō: Passages Deploring Deviations of Faith	
106-I	*Jp.*	Ren-nyo-shō-nin-o-fumi （蓮如上人御文）	2668
	Eng.	Rennyo Shōnin Ofumi: The Letters of Rennyo	
106-II	*Jp.*	Ō-jō-yō-shū （往生要集）	2682
107-I	*Jp.*	Has-shū-kō-yō （八宗綱要）	蔵外
	Eng.	The Essentials of the Eight Traditions	
107-II	*Jp.*	San-gō-shī-ki （三教指帰）	蔵外
107-III	*Jp.*	Map-pō-tō-myō-ki （末法燈明記）	蔵外
	Eng.	The Candle of the Latter Dharma	
107-IV	*Jp.*	Jū-shichi-jō-ken-pō （十七條憲法）	蔵外